# Backyard Foraging

# Backyard Foraging

## 65 Familiar Plants
## You Didn't Know You Could Eat

Ellen Zachos

Storey Publishing

The mission of Storey Publishing is to serve our customers by
publishing practical information that encourages
personal independence in harmony with the environment.

Edited by Carleen Madigan
Art direction and book design by Mary Winkelman Velgos
Text production by Liseann Karandisecky

Cover photography by © Rob Cardillo, except for front, top by Mars Vilaubi
Interior photography credits appear on page 229

Indexed by Andrea Chesman

Eating wild plants and fungi is inherently risky. Individual people may make mistaken
identifications regardless of their level of expertise or the accuracy of printed information,
and they also vary in their physiological reactions. The publisher and the author cannot
accept responsibility for their health. Readers eat wild foods at their own risk.

**Storey books are available at special discounts** when purchased in bulk for premiums and
sales promotions as well as for fund-raising or educational use. Special editions or book
excerpts can also be created to specification. For details, please call 800-827-8673, or send
an email to sales@storey.com.

**Storey Publishing**
210 MASS MoCA Way
North Adams, MA 01247
*www.storey.com*

Printed in the United States by Versa Press
20  19  18  17  16  15  14  13  12  11  10

Library of Congress Cataloging-in-Publication

Zachos, Ellen.
  Backyard foraging / by Ellen Zachos.
    pages cm
  Includes index.
  ISBN 978-1-61212-009-6 (pbk. : alk. paper)
  ISBN 978-1-60342-849-1 (ebook)
  1.  Wild plants, Edible—Identification. 2.  Cooking (Wild foods) I. Title.
QK98.5.A1Z33 2013
641.3'03—dc23
                              2012043352

No one learns to forage on their own. This book is dedicated to the friends who have taught me and the friends I have taught. Mark, Leda, Cayce, and Michael — here's to many more years of foraging, cooking, and eating together.

What a pleasure to work with a photographer and an editor who enjoy wild edibles! Thanks to Rob Cardillo for making art out of the ordinary, and for being willing to try everything I asked him to eat. Thanks to Carleen Madigan for her sharp editorial eye, her plant suggestions, and for the nuts and berries she foraged and sent my way. Many thanks also to my crew of dedicated readers: Michael, John, and Elizabeth. I feel safe in your hands.

# INTRODUCTION

"But how do you know it's safe?"

Jacob was not about to accept my offer of ripe Juneberries without a little more information. We were hiking in the White Mountains of New Hampshire, miles away from the nearest grocery store, and as far as my nephew was concerned, the woods were not for eating. I showed him the five-pointed crown on the top of the berry, and explained that any berry with that feature was safe to eat. I showed him the tree it came from (an *Amelanchier* species) and its characteristic smooth gray bark and oval leaves. I cut open a berry with my fingernail to show him the small seeds dispersed throughout. Finally, I ate a few of the berries myself.

When I didn't immediately keel over or grab my stomach in anguish, Jacob decided to trust me, but he was right to ask questions. The first rule of foraging is never, *ever,* eat anything you're not 100 percent sure of. This applies whether

Ripe Juneberries are a juicy treat found in yards, parks, and woodlands.

you're picking in the wild or in your own backyard.

*"Foraging in your own backyard!"* you say. "I thought you had to wander the fields and woods to forage." Nope. Truth is, many of our favorite garden plants have edible parts that have simply been overlooked. And since many of us already know what we're growing in our own backyards, identification there is a lot easier than it would be in the wild. It's a great way to

start foraging and to introduce new edible plants to your menu.

This book presents familiar ornamental plants and weeds with a secret: they just happen to be delicious. Each plant has its own profile, with information on how it grows, how to harvest it while preserving its ornamental value (or how to control its weediness), and how to best use it in the kitchen. You'll see plants in the

My fall harvest bowl includes wintergreen, black walnuts, canna rhizomes, silverberries, and hopniss tubers.

landscape, in close-up, and as food.

But wait, there's more! By going one step further and actually planting your garden with edible ornamentals, you can make the most out of your space, even if it's very small. Historically, gardeners have considered ornamental plants (trees, shrubs, vines, perennials, and annuals) as separate from edible plants (fruits, vegetables, and herbs) and have planted them in different locations. Do you have the time and energy to plant separate kitchen and ornamental gardens, replete with stylish tuteurs and weeded paths? Do you have enough space to plant two different kinds of gardens? I don't.

I look at ornamental plants with edible parts as the superheroes of the modern garden. They feed body and soul (with their deliciousness and beauty, respectively) and cut back on gardening chores by letting you focus your precious time on a single space.

"But," you argue, "a quick trip to the supermarket is so fast and easy, why take time to walk around the backyard, looking for food?" Because it's there. Because it's free. And because it's fun. The thrill of discovery (*you can eat that?*) is intoxicating!

Let's walk around the neighborhood. I'll show you the best leaves for salad and the tastiest berries to snack on. Deliciousness is key. This is not a field guide or a survival manual. Sure, it's fun to imagine which wild plants you might live on if you got lost in the woods, but if this stuff weren't tasty, I wouldn't be interested. I'm not sure why today's gardener has forgotten that daylily buds and milkweed pods are astonishingly delicious, but it's time to get reacquainted with these excellent vegetables.

What if you don't have your own garden? Don't despair! Perhaps you have friendly neighbors who'd be happy to have a jar of Oregon grape jelly in exchange for letting you forage in their backyard. Whenever you're foraging on private property, be sure you ask permission first, even if you're only removing the occasional dandelion. It's also possible to forage in public places when you know the rules. For example, the National Park Service allows individuals to pick up to 25 pounds of pine nuts per year, as long as they're for noncommercial use and no trees are damaged in the picking. While most parks don't allow wholesale harvesting of leaves and stems, they're more relaxed about nuts and berries. Collecting mushrooms and weeds may also be permitted; just be sure to ask first.

Which brings me back to the ease and elegance of *backyard foraging*. You've already got permission, and you probably know what you're growing. So let's get started!

# CHAPTER 1

# GETTING STARTED:
# Identifying Habitats in the 'Hood

A crop of large, luscious rose hips is just beginning to ripen.

*Wild foods,* nontraditional edibles, foraged foods — whatever you call them, these comestibles have much to recommend them. Sure, backyard foraging reduces your carbon footprint, but the key reason for eating these plants is that they taste great. Their surprising flavors, unusual textures, fresh colors, and nutritional value can liven up your cooking, or offer convenient snacking right from your own backyard.

Different landscapes produce different plants. Take a look around and assess your surroundings. Where are you? What do you see?

*Are you standing on a mowed lawn?* Get down on your hands and knees to look for sheep sorrel, chickweed, dandelion, and pineapple weed.

*Is there a meadow behind your house?* Poke around in the high grasses to look for milkweed, wild garlic, and oxeye daisies, and check the meadow's edges for silverberry, sweetfern, chestnut, and black walnut.

*Are you sitting pretty on a few wooded acres?* Look for spicebush, Juneberry, garlic mustard, wild ginger, ostrich fern, miner's lettuce, wintergreen, mayapple, sassafras, or California bay.

Automobile pollution can be absorbed by roadside plants, so watch where you pick.

*Are you near a stream, river, or lake?*
Look for hopniss, chokeberry, or Japanese knotweed.

*Are you looking at a vacant lot that's weedy and overgrown?*
This could be the perfect place for sumac, purslane, or Japanese knotweed.

In an urban park you might find garlic mustard, milkweed, miner's lettuce, ginkgo nuts, daylilies, dandelions, and elderberries.

## Ensuring Safety

Wherever your food comes from, you want to know that it's clean and healthy. If you buy an apple at the grocery store, you probably wash it before taking a bite. You trust that the land where it grew was safe for farming — i.e., not contaminated with waste or heavy metals. If it's an organic apple, you know that whoever grew it didn't spray the fruit with anything toxic or harmful. These same concerns and questions apply to foraging.

## In Your Backyard

You should know what's been sprayed on your own plants, in your own backyard. Do you use weed killers to produce a prize-winning lawn? Maybe you've sprayed an insecticide to keep aphids off your roses. You need to look closely at the labels of any product you've applied to see if it's toxic. If it is, you'll need to do a little research to determine if and when you can safely eat something that's been sprayed.

## In Public Places

If you're harvesting in a park (with permission, of course), you should inquire about its spraying policy. Often, rural parks have a no-spray policy, preferring to let nature reign supreme. City parks may spray, but they generally post signs immediately before and after, explaining which chemicals have been used and where. If your yard is adjacent to a park, a golf course, agricultural fields, or timber property, it

**A FEW REMINDERS**
Remember these points, and you should be able to forage safely, within the law, and without ticking off the neighbors:

- Be 100 percent certain of what you're picking. I've said it before, and I'll say it again. And again. And again.
- Avoid foraging from ground polluted by pesticides, insecticides, animals, automobiles, or manufacturing.
- Try every new food in moderation.
- Don't overharvest.
- If you're foraging on land you don't own, ask permission of private property owners and learn the relevant rules about picking on public land.

may be susceptible to drift from herbicides and insecticides.

High-traffic roadsides and parking lots aren't the best places to harvest edibles. Pollutants from automobile exhaust can be absorbed from both the air and soil by plant roots and leaves. These can't be washed away or cooked out of the plant. How far from the road it is safe to harvest depends on the terrain, how busy the road is, and what you're picking. Here are a few tips:

- Give yourself a distance of 100 feet from a well-traveled road or highway. If it's a quiet gravel road in the countryside, 15 or 20 feet should suffice.

- Land uphill from a road is less likely to be contaminated by exhaust than land that is the same distance downhill from the road. As particles settle out of exhaust and fall to the ground, they tend to move downhill, not up.

- Animal waste may be a problem in yards, parks, and city tree pits (those mini-gardens that surround city trees), but this can be washed away, unlike heavy metals that might be absorbed by plant roots.

- Root crops are most likely to contain soil contaminants because they are storage organs. They store nutrition for the plant (and inadvertently for us), and toxins may also be stored in their tissues.

## Allergy Awareness

The first time you try *any* new food, whether it's foraged from your backyard or picked from the produce bins at Whole Foods, try a small amount. This way, if you meet up with a food that doesn't agree with you or discover an actual allergy, the reaction will be minimized. A taste of something may be disagreeable, but a plateful might send you to the emergency room. If you *know* you have food allergies, it's a good idea to avoid eating plants closely related to the allergens. For example, sumac is in the same family (Anacardiaceae) as mangoes and cashews, and thus may provoke a similar allergic reaction. Wintergreen contains methyl salicylate, which is closely related to salicylic acid, the main ingredient in aspirin. If aspirin doesn't agree with you, go easy on the wintergreen.

## Ethical Harvesting

When harvesting, please consider the welfare of the plant in addition to your own well-being. Unless you're picking weeds, don't overharvest. This means different things for different plants. If you're picking fiddleheads, you should never take more than three from each fern. Overpicking leaves the plant too weak to thrive. If you're pinching the top leaves off an invasive chameleon plant, you can pretty much go to town. Abundant berries and nuts are hard to resist, but do leave some behind for the birds. With root crops, be sure to leave enough to sprout the following year.

Masses of miner's lettuce blanket this San Francisco hillside. Who's going to miss a few leaves?

## FORAGING QUIZ

Now that you have a general operating procedure, take a look around your neighborhood at a few potential foraging spots. Should you harvest from these places?

**The spot:** A perfectly groomed public rose garden with nary a black spot or yellow leaf.
**A:** Just walk away.

**The spot:** A path to the beach, lined with wild roses that are full of plump, ripe, red rose hips.
**A:** Ask permission first, but these are probably okay to harvest.

**The spot:** Your neighbor's shade garden, which is bursting with fiddlehead ferns.
**A:** If the plants are plentiful, your neighbor may let you pick a few, but why not plant your own?

**The spot:** The lawn in Central Park, which is covered with stinky fallen ginkgo fruit.
**A:** Gather to your heart's content. Nuts that have fallen to the ground are generally fair game. And in this case, many people would consider it a public service!

**The spot:** Your knotweed-filled camp-site near the Delaware River.
**A:** Harvest away!

# CHAPTER 2

# HARVEST WITH CARE:
# You Don't Have to Sacrifice Your Scenery

Grate a few magnolia buds for an unusual spice and leave the rest to flower in your garden.

**When you grow** tomatoes, you don't necessarily care what the plants look like as long as the fruit is juicy and sweet. Good thing, because tomato plants often look pretty beat by the end of the summer. But when you're eating your ornamental garden, appearances *do* matter. It's important to know how and when to harvest your food and still keep things looking pretty.

Each ornamental edible has an appropriate harvest time, just like traditional edibles. You wouldn't pick a peach when it's green and hard, and you shouldn't harvest your Juneberries while they're still red. Learning when to pick each edible will ensure you enjoy your harvest at its peak. The timing depends on what you're picking and how you plan to use it.

A leaf node is the place on the stem of a plant from which a leaf emerges.

## Picking Shoots and Young Foliage

When picking young shoots of plants like hostas, you should cut from around the outside of the clump, snipping new growth just above the soil line. As the remaining leaves unfurl, they'll cover the cut stems and the plant will look whole. The same technique can be applied to daylily shoots. Both hostas and daylilies produce enough shoots from a single crown that you can harvest up to 25 percent without weakening the plant or marring its appearance.

Some edible leaf crops should be picked after they have unfurled. If each leaf emerges from the ground on its own stem, cut the stem at soil level. If multiples leaves grow from a single stem, make your cut just above a leaf node (see image above).

You don't want to leave leafless stems behind; it just doesn't look good. If the crop in question is a weed (garlic mustard, miner's lettuce, purslane), pick to your heart's content. If the leaves are highly ornamental, limit yourself to a taste that won't spoil your garden's appearance. Just as you might pinch the top few leaves off a coleus or basil plant to keep it neat and shapely, you can pick tender new leaves of nasturtium, Malabar spinach, or bee balm. You'll be grooming your plants and harvesting edibles at the same time.

A member of the mint family, bee balm sometimes spreads overenthusiastically. If this is the case in your garden, you can harvest by pulling up young shoots.

## Foraging Flowers, Fruits, and Nuts

Flowers are tricky; pick too many and you'll reduce your fruit crop later in the growing season. If you're picking spring elderflowers for fritters or champagne, leave enough to be pollinated and provide berries in fall. Other flowers are produced so abundantly (and don't ripen into edible fruits) that they can be harvested in great number. Daylilies, lilacs, redbuds, and dandelions are good examples.

Fruit is often highly ornamental in addition to being delicious. Some plants produce so much fruit (like silverberries, spicebush, and crab apples) you can harvest as much as you want and still leave plenty on the shrubs to brighten up the landscape. Other plants produce a more limited crop and you'll want to pick it all; Juneberries, chokeberries, and Oregon grapes fall into this category. Enjoy the beauty of the fruit while it ripens and develops color, then harvest when it's at its peak. True, you

Oregon grapes are extremely sour but make an excellent jelly.

may miss the seductive clusters of deep purple elderberries hanging heavy on their branches, but when you're sipping elderberry wine or spreading elderberry jelly on toasted scones, the sacrifice will seem worthwhile.

Nuts are easy to harvest but difficult to process. They obligingly fall to the ground when ripe, making gathering the crop a straightforward task. The post-harvest processing is where the work comes in; many nuts require shelling and curing before they can be eaten. But since nuts are especially tasty and highly nutritious, you may decide they're worth the extra work.

## SAME AS STORE-BOUGHT?

What's the difference between a blueberry from the grocery store and a blueberry from a bush in your own backyard? No difference at all — and all the difference in the world.

No difference at all, because the shrubs that bear the fruit are the same species of shrub, producing the same species of fruit. All the difference in the world, because when you harvest your own fruit, it tastes better. But beyond the emotional preference of a devoted gardener or forager, there may be some actual, physical differences between the two fruits that explain why homegrown often tastes better.

Commercially raised fruits are regularly irrigated and fertilized. They are also harvested slightly before peak ripeness. Ripe fruit is softer and doesn't ship as well as slightly underripe fruit. Shipping underripe fruit means berries arrive in better condition and with a longer shelf life. But a berry that ripens on the shelf will never taste as good as a berry that ripens in the sun. Fruit picked from your backyard will be harvested at its peak: sweet, soft, and bursting with flavor.

Additionally, berries grown with less than perfect irrigation and fertilization may be smaller and sweeter. I'm not suggesting that, if you're growing fruit, you should stress your fruit on purpose. Nor am I saying your irrigation and fertilization routines are imperfect. But if they are, take heart! Many growers believe that a little dryness at the right stage of berry development concentrates the flavor and makes for a tastier, albeit smaller, berry. But be careful; withholding moisture at the wrong stage of development may cause fruit to abort.

The truth is that many of the fruits, vegetables, herbs, nuts, and mushrooms we find on supermarket shelves are essentially the same as those we find in our backyards and neighborhood parks. The differences are subtle but important. Whether you taste the difference or not, I bet you'll enjoy eating the oyster mushroom you picked from the stump in your backyard a lot more than the oyster mushroom you picked from the produce bin at Whole Foods.

## Digging Roots and Tubers

Root crops must be harvested with an eye toward preserving the plant population. You'll want to leave enough behind to ensure the plants come back the following year. Since many roots are harvested at the end of the growing season, collecting them can be part of your winter garden prep. Dig up the plant as if you're going to divide it, then remove a quarter to half of the tubers, bulbs, or stolons for consumption. How much you replant will depend on how fast the plant grows and how much of it you want in your garden next year.

Roots and tubers are best picked when their leaves and stems are not in active growth. This may be at the end of the growing season, when top growth is dormant and belowground tissue is plump and full after a season's worth of production and storage, or in early spring, before the plant has tapped the reserve nutrition stored in its belowground tissue. If the plant is in active growth, depleting that stored nutrition, your crop will be disappointing.

These dahlia tubers can be either planted or eaten. Raw they taste somewhat like radishes.

## Timing for Taste

Gardeners watch their plants grow from young shoots to mature plants, through flowering, fruiting, and setting seed. They learn to recognize and appreciate the different stages of growth and understand what each plant needs as it moves through the growing season.

Foraging is the ultimate in seasonal eating, and following a plant through the seasons makes you a savvier forager. You can't wake up one October morning and decide you want to harvest mayapples . . . they won't be there! Nor will you be able to pick Japanese quince fruit in April. But you *can* appreciate the quince's flowers in spring, knowing that, come October, its fruit will be ready and ripe for the picking.

Stems and leafy greens are generally best eaten young, for several reasons. New,

Fiddleheads should be harvested when they're still tightly furled. These have passed their edible prime.

tender leaves and shoots may be eaten raw in early spring, but they require cooking later in the season when they develop stronger fibers in their foliage. The fibers don't make these leaves inedible, but they do make them a little tougher. The mature plant will be more palatable if it's chopped and cooked. Other leaf crops develop bitter compounds in the heat, drought, and full sun of summer. For example, both dandelions and garlic mustard may be slightly bitter in spring and fall, offering a nice sharpness when used with other raw greens in salads. In July or August those same plants are often too bitter to be eaten raw, unless they're grown in moist, shady conditions. Steaming or boiling removes some of the bitter compounds at this stage of growth. Lemon juice and olive oil improve the taste even further.

Fall fruits are often sweeter after a light frost, but they'll have more pectin (a natural jelling agent, crucial for jelly making) if you pick them early, slightly underripe. Of course the longer you leave fruit on the tree, the greater the chance that the birds or squirrels will beat you to them.

Ask yourself these questions before harvesting:

- How much of the plant can I pick and still have it look nice?

- When is the edible part at its most delicious?

- How do I want to prepare this food?

When you know the answers, it should be easy to have your garden and eat it, too.

## WEATHER REPORT

Most people won't want to be outside, poking around in the garden in the middle of a rainstorm, but foraging *after* the rain is an excellent idea for several reasons.

If you're combining chores and want to harvest edible weeds from your garden, it's easier to pull them after a rain, when the soil is moist. In fact, if you haven't had rain, it's a good idea to run a sprinkler the night before you plan to weed, just to moisten the soil. Moist soil is more elastic and easier to work with. You'll also have a better chance of getting the whole root system out when it's flexible and full of moisture. Dry, brittle roots may break apart, leaving behind a piece that will continue to grow.

There's a difference between moist soil and wet soil. It's not a good idea to work in the garden when the soil is wet. (If you can pick up a clod of soil and squeeze water out of it, go back inside and cook something.) You risk compressing wet soil by walking or kneeling on it, and wet soil will cling to roots in large clods. If you've cultivated this soil, spending precious hours amending it with compost and TLC, you won't want to undo all that. The idea is to remove weeds, not soil, so wait until the soil has gone from wet to moist.

Mushrooms require lots of moisture to sprout; you won't find many during hot, dry weather, which is why fall is such a productive time for mushroom hunting. Plentiful autumn rains give fungi the moisture they need for rapid growth. A few days after a good soaking rain is the perfect time to look for fresh mushrooms.

Once again, there's a fine line between just enough and too much. Fresh mushrooms are moist and soft; too much rain can cause them to disintegrate, melting into a mushy mass of wasted fungal flesh. So time your harvest carefully. A few days after a rain is a good time to look. If you put off the hunt and it starts to rain again, you may have missed your chance.

These hen-of-the-woods mushrooms grow quickly in moist fall weather.

# Tools of the Trade

No matter what you're doing, it's important to have the right tool for the job; the right tool can turn a lengthy task into a quick project. Here's a list that will help simplify the harvest and preparation of your backyard buffet.

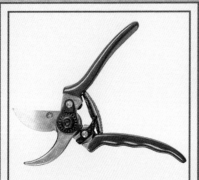

## Bypass pruners

If you have a garden or do regular yard work, you probably already have a set of pruners. If you don't, and you're going shopping for a pair, make sure to buy bypass pruners instead of anvil pruners. Bypass pruners have one sharp blade that slides by another to make the cut, whereas anvil pruners have a single sharp blade that applies pressure against a flat, anvil-shaped surface. Anvil pruners require less hand strength, but they crush the stem of the plant being cut, so they aren't good for pruning stems or branches that you hope will continue to grow. If you're chopping up dead branches for the compost pile, anvil pruners are fine.

## Garden fork

A garden fork is similar to a pitchfork but has more prongs (four instead of three) and a shorter handle. It's also slightly sturdier, intended for turning and sifting soil rather than lifting and tossing lightweight objects like hay. Garden forks are perfect for harvesting underground crops such as tubers. While you could use a spade to dig up your Jerusalem artichokes, cannas, dahlias, or hopniss, a garden fork makes the task easier because you're not lifting out big shovel-fuls of heavy soil. Push the tines into the soil and turn to break apart the earth, then reveal your crop. Also, there's less chance you'll cut a tuber in half with a garden fork than with a spade.

## Transplant spade

A transplant spade is specially shaped for transplanting perennials, shrubs, and trees. You may still need to use a little muscle, depending on the job, but the long, narrow blade of the spade lets you get down deep, underneath the rootball, with less effort than with a traditional shovel or spade. A long-handled model will give you more leverage than a spade with a shorter handle. This may come in handy digging up giant clumps of hostas or daylilies; those rootballs can be large and heavy!

## Pocket knife

A knife is necessary for cutting mushrooms off trees cleanly, without tearing the bark. When you're harvesting mushrooms from the ground, slicing the stem with a knife gives you a cleaner harvest. Pulling up the entire mushroom often delivers dirt and leaves along with your fungi, which makes cleaning them later a more onerous task.

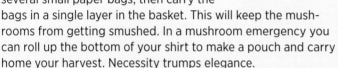

## Collecting bags and basket

If you're out looking for mushrooms, take along several small paper or wax-paper bags and a basket. Mushrooms are delicate creatures and shouldn't be jostled about or piled too heavily on top of each other. Instead, divide your harvest among several small paper bags, then carry the bags in a single layer in the basket. This will keep the mushrooms from getting smushed. In a mushroom emergency you can roll up the bottom of your shirt to make a pouch and carry home your harvest. Necessity trumps elegance.

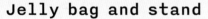

## Food mill

Some fruits (Juneberries and mulberries) have small seeds you won't mind eating. Others (cornelian cherries and Oregon grape) have large seeds that would seriously impair your eating enjoyment. A brief simmer softens the fruit, which you can then pass through a food mill, separating the seeds from the juice and pulp. Look for a food mill with interchangeable plates of different-size holes. You'll want to use the plate with the largest possible hole that will still catch the seeds while letting the pulp and juice pass through. The smaller the hole, the harder you'll have to turn the mill.

## Jelly bag and stand

It's possible to use a strainer lined with cheesecloth to process fruit juice, but I like a dedicated jelly bag for several reasons. First, jelly bags tend to be long and narrow, and the extra weight of the vertically packed fruit makes extracting the juice faster. Second, the defined shape of a jelly bag and its tight fit over a jelly-bag stand makes for fewer accidents. A piece of cheese-cloth can slide around on a strainer,  letting fruit pulp and seeds pass through into the juice. Third, jelly bags are almost infinitely reusable, while the loose weave of cheesecloth makes it difficult to clean and more likely to tear. I've been using the same jelly bag for 10 years and it shows no signs of age.

## Canning jars

Whether you're pressure-canning or canning in a boiling water bath, you'll need special jars with two-part lids that create a vacuum seal to keep your food safe. Ball jars, a common brand, are ubiquitous and generally the least expensive. They come in narrow- and wide-mouth styles and a variety of sizes and shapes from half gallons to quarter pints. Ball also makes several interesting shapes and sizes that are especially nice for gifts. Weck, a German company, makes canning jars that are so beautiful it hurts me to look at them. They are also so expensive I've never bought them. Weck jars use a system of glass lids with rubber gaskets and metal clamps. Someday I'll treat myself to a few Weck jars, although I'm not sure I'll be able to use them for gifts because I won't want to give them away, except to those family members who loyally return their gift jars to me every year. I like to think they do it because they want refills.

## Spice grinder

Yes, you could chop your spices with a knife or grind them with a mortar and pestle. I use a coffee bean grinder to grind fresh, dried, or frozen spices (like wild ginger, juniper berries, and spicebush berries) in a flash. So! Much! Easier! Of course I don't grind coffee beans in this grinder; their strong taste would carry over to the spices. The spices have their own dedicated grinder.

## Food dehydrator

If you have an oven that can be set very low (125°F), you may not need a dehydrator. But most ovens don't go below 150°F, so you end up propping the door open to get temperatures appropriate for dehydrating. I'm not comfortable with this kind of inefficiency. Depending on the model, dehydrators can be set for anywhere from 90 to 150°F. You'll use the lower temperatures for drying leaves and flower petals and the higher temperatures for fruits, fruit leathers, and mushrooms. Dehydrators use much less energy than stoves. Also many have timers, making them very convenient. Special nonstick sheets (for making fruit leather) can be ordered to fit the dehydrating trays.

## Boiling water bath canner

If you're only going to make a few jars of jam or jelly every year, you probably don't need a dedicated canner. You can process pint or half-pint jars in a large pasta pot, as long as you can cover the tops of the jars with 2 inches of water. It's also a good idea to put a folded-up dishtowel on the bottom of the pot so the jars don't crack while jostling around in the boiling water. If you fall in love with canning (it's an addictive hobby), you'll want to buy a larger canning rig that accommodates quart jars and has a rack that makes for easy lifting in and out of the boiling water.

## Pressure canner

While jams, jellies, and pickles can be canned in a boiling water bath, low-acid foods need to be canned under pressure for safe preservation. If you want to can a bumper crop of milkweed pods or several extra quarts of mushroom soup, you'll need a pressure canner. This is different from a pressure cooker, which is a vessel intended to cook foods under pressure (i.e., faster than you'd be able to cook them normally). People use pressure cookers to speed the preparation of beans, lentils, and meats that generally require long cooking times. You can use a pressure canner for pressure cooking, but not always vice versa. Most pressure cookers are too small to accommodate the height of quart jars.

# CHAPTER 3

# GRAZING GREENS:
# Tasty Leaves and Stems

The tart leaves of oxeye daisy make an excellent salad green.

# When you walk through your garden, you see woody plants

(trees, shrubs, and vines) and herbaceous plants (perennials, biennials, and annuals). Both provide edible greens. Some greens are tasty all season long, while others have shorter seasons of deliciousness. Each plant profile in this chapter includes information on the best time to harvest. If you know which plant parts are in season when, you'll be able to collect each crop in its prime.

People don't generally eat woody stems, but the leaves of woody plants can be tasty when they're young and tender. Harvest hemlock and spruce needles in spring, when they are flavorful and light green. Leaves of the sweet fern shrub are useful all season long, as are the evergreen leaves of wintergreen, a woody ground cover. Sassafras leaves are useful for most of the growing season, until they turn color in fall.

Herbaceous plants (those that die back to the ground in winter) provide edible stems and leaves, sometimes both on a single plant! While leaves are generally edible as long as they're tender, some develop a bitter taste or tough fibers during the growing season. Stems (also called stalks or shoots) are tastiest while still young and tender.

SPRING   SUMMER   FALL   WINTER

# BAMBOO

## *Phyllostachys* species

**What it is:** an attractive, invasive, delicious member of the grass family
**Where to find it:** anywhere except very dry soils
**Edible parts:** young shoots

## THE DETAILS

Not all bamboo is invasive, but all *Phyllostachys* species are; these are running (not clumping) bamboos. This is not a plant for a small garden!

Pick these shoots now, before they take over the universe!

If you plant one, use industrial-strength underground barriers manufactured specifically to keep running bamboo in check. And if you happen to find a giant clump in your new backyard, you may be able to keep it under control by eating the new shoots before they have a chance to spread. This genus produces some of the loveliest ornamentals and some of the tastiest shoots, such as golden bamboo (*P. aurea*), sweet shoot bamboo (*P. dulcis*), moso (*P. edulis*), waxy blue bamboo (*P. nigra* 'Henon'), and zigzag bamboo (*P. flexuosa*). The height of the mature plants and the diameter of the edible shoots vary according to species; all of them grow well in sun to part shade with moderate moisture.

## HOW TO HARVEST

Shoots are tastiest and most tender when they are 6 to 12 inches tall. Because bamboo is an extremely fast grower, you have to be on the lookout. It can emerge from the ground and grow 6 inches in a single day. Shoots can also be harvested before they emerge from the ground. If you notice soil bulging up in the bamboo grove, gently poke around until you feel a shoot, and cut it as far below the soil as you can reach. Since running bamboos are difficult to control, it is highly unlikely you will over-harvest this plant.

## HOW TO EAT IT

Bamboo shoots should be boiled before eating. Some species contain a toxic cyanogenic glyco-side called taxiphyllin. Fortunately, taxiphyllin is reliably removed by boiling, so any bamboo shoot should be safe to eat when properly prepared. The size of your shoot will affect how long it must be boiled, but the procedure is the same for any shoot.

From left to right: raw, unpeeled shoots; boiled, unpeeled shoots; boiled, peeled shoots (ready for eating).

First, cut the pointy tip off the shoot. Next, with a sharp knife slice through the outer skin of the shoot, being careful not to go deeper than one-third of the way through the shoot. Boil the shoots until they are tender enough to be punctured with a chopstick (start checking the thinnest shoots after about 15 minutes). Remove tender shoots from the water, and let them cool.

Asian recipes often suggest boiling the shoots with rice bran, to remove bitterness from the shoot. I have never had rice bran on hand, nor have I ever found my bamboo shoots to be bitter. But bitterness varies from species to species, so if you do get a bitter shoot, consider the rice bran method.

When the shoots have cooled, peel away the outer layers (there will be several) until you reach the smooth, slippery core of the shoot. Slice it up to add to salads, rice dishes, and stir-fries. To get the pure taste of bamboo, try one plain. They are so delicious, they may not make it to the dinner table. And bamboo shoots are an excellent source of fiber.

SPRING   SUMMER   FALL   WINTER

# BEE BALM

## *Monarda didyma* and *M. fistulosa*

**What it is:** garden perennial
**Where to find it:** sun to part sun; gardens, fields
**Edible parts:** leaves and flower petals

### THE DETAILS

Bee balm is a popular garden plant, with flowers available in red, pink, magenta, white, or blue-purple. New hybrids are being bred with better resistance to powdery mildew, a fungal disease that mars the foliage and makes it inedible. Powdery mildew is problematic in humid locations with low air circulation, but with careful siting and thinning of the plant you should be able to avoid the problem. Since bee balm is a member of the mint family, both the foliage and flowers are highly fragrant and useful as herbs.

### HOW TO HARVEST

Both leaves and flowers have a strong, oregano-like flavor. Pick flowers when they are newly opened. The individual tube-shaped petals can be chopped and used as an herb; whole flowers can be steeped in vinegar, where they will impart both flavor and color. Red flowers make the most striking vinegar. Pinch young leaves from the tops of plants and chop them finely to use in any way you'd use oregano. Both foliage and flowers can be used fresh or dried.

### HOW TO EAT IT

Another common name for bee balm is bergamot. The bergamot orange is used to flavor Earl Grey tea, and some people think the flavor of bee balm resembles that of Earl Grey. Personally, I don't taste the resemblance, but I admit that bee balm makes a superior tea, hot or iced. Use bee balm vinegar to create an interesting vinaigrette or to add a unique taste to pickles. The chopped flowers and leaves are an excellent herb to use on pasta, rice, or pizza; in tomato sauces, focaccia, or bruschetta; or in a dry rub for meats and fish. Bee balm is a versatile herb with a warm, spicy taste.

Try using bee balm leaves instead of oregano when you're cooking.

These bright red flowers add both color and spice to your cooking.

SPRING    SUMMER    FALL    WINTER

# BISHOP'S WEED, GOUTWEED
## *Aegopodium podagraria*

**What it is:** attractive, aggressive ground cover, often deeply regretted
**Where to find it:** sun or shade; moist soils
**Edible parts:** leaves

## THE DETAILS

I planted bishop's weed in several places when we moved into our house, well aware that most people think of it as a bully in the garden. I needed ground cover and I needed it fast. While some people might consider this a mistake, I went in with my eyes wide open. I knew it was a garden thug, but I also knew I could eat it. Most garden centers sell the variegated variety, despite the plant being listed as a noxious weed in 46 states. A solid green variety of bishop's weed grows even faster (the horror!) and is also edible.

## HOW TO HARVEST

Don't hold back. This plant spreads by underground rhizomes. Zealous harvesting will cause only a slight hiccup in growth.

Any piece of rhizome left beneath the soil will quickly put out new leaves. To harvest, pinch or cut stems at soil level, then separate the leaf and stem, discarding the stem and saving the leaf. The stem can be composted if it's free of roots, but if not, you may find bishop's weed covering the top your compost pile. When in doubt, bag the leftover pieces in your trash. Many gardeners have tried to eliminate this aggressive perennial from their garden, consumed by regret at having planted it in the first place. I've been able to keep it in bounds by judicious harvesting and eating.

Some people think the foliage tastes slightly bitter after flowers develop, although I have not found this to be true.

If you're concerned about it, though, you can prevent flowering by shearing off the bloom spikes as they appear in early to midsummer.

## HOW TO EAT IT

Young leaves are an attractive addition to salads. Their taste is light, fresh, and vegetal, with a hint of celery. This is a mild-tasting green, though the solid green variety has a slightly stronger flavor. New foliage will be more

Mature foliage can be used as a spinach substitute and makes an excellent filling for a Greek *pita*. (*Pita* is the Greek word for pie.)

attractive (glossy and unblemished), as well as more tender. New leaves emerge throughout the growing season.

Mature foliage can be used as a spinach substitute and makes an excellent filling for a Greek *pita*. (*Pita* is the Greek word for pie.) While spanakopita has made the transition to roadside diner fare, its more authentic cousin hortopita remains uncelebrated . . . until now. *Horta* is the Greek word for greens, and Greeks make *pites* (plural of pita) from whatever greens are on hand. My *yiayia* (grandmother) grew up in the mountains of central Greece, where wild edibles were an important part of village diets. The villagers would mix and match as needed, add a little cheese, some onions, a few herbs, and call it pita. (See hortopita recipe on page 221.) Since bishop's weed usually grows in abundance, it shouldn't be hard to harvest enough for an entire pie. Its leaves can also be used as chopped greens in soups.

Bishop's weed is a very aggressive grower. You can limit its run by planting it between a rock and a hard place . . . or a stone wall and a flagstone path.

SPRING  SUMMER  FALL  WINTER

# CALIFORNIA BAY, OREGON MYRTLE

## *Umbellularia californica*

**What it is:** a large evergreen tree
**Where to find it:** gardens, woods, and roadsides of coastal California and Oregon
**Edible parts:** leaves, ripe nuts

This lovely shade tree provides spicy leaves and irresistible nuts.

## THE DETAILS

While the native region of this tree is limited, it adapts well to garden culture and can either become a large specimen tree or be kept pruned to an easily harvestable height. It grows best in full sun to part shade and is fairly drought tolerant once established. Its fragrant, evergreen leaves are similar in appearance to those of the traditional bay tree (*Laurus nobilis*) but are stronger in taste. An East Coast native, bayberry (*Myrica pensylvanica*) is also sometimes used as a bay leaf substitute, although its foliage has a milder scent and flavor.

## HOW TO HARVEST

Snip green leaves above a leaf node and use them fresh or dried in any recipe

Inside the green-and-yellow fruits hide tasty nut meats.

that calls for traditional bay leaf. Leaves can be harvested as long as they're entirely green and pliable.

Bay nuts are enclosed in a fruit that resembles a small avocado — in color and texture, but certainly not in taste! The fruit starts out green and can be picked when it turns yellow. It will fall from the tree at about the same time the flesh turns purple. At this stage the fruit is rotting and will be less pleasant to handle. Slice around the fruit with a sharp knife, peel back the flesh, and discard. (Trust me, unless you're starving, throw it away. Despite hearing several accounts of tasty fruit, I have never found it palatable.) Let the nuts dry for a week or two at room temperature, then roast on a cookie sheet at 350°F for just over a half hour. If you try to take a shortcut and roast without drying, you may hear explosions coming from inside your oven. Bye-bye nut meat.

## HOW TO EAT IT

Substitute the leaves of California bay for traditional bay leaves, but remember their flavor is considerably stronger. Bite into a fresh leaf to see what I mean. I suggest starting with a quarter of the recommended amount and tweaking according to your taste.

Bay nuts have an intriguing taste. I kept reading about their being bitter and tasting like burnt popcorn, neither of which made me want to run right out and harvest a bunch. Curiosity got the better of me, and I'm glad it did. The roasted nuts are easily removed from their thin shells. Their texture is soft and crumbly. Yes, the nuts are slightly bitter, but in a black coffee kind of way. Combine them with brown sugar and oatmeal for a fruit crisp topping, or stir the chopped nuts into melted dark chocolate (equal parts) and freeze spoonfuls of the mixture on a cookie sheet covered with wax paper. The flavors complement each other wonderfully and leave me wanting more.

> Substitute the leaves of California bay for traditional bay leaves, but remember their flavor is considerably stronger.

# CHAMELEON PLANT

## *Houttuynia cordata* 'Chameleon' and other variegated varieties

**What it is:** an aggressive (and very pretty) perennial ground cover
**Where to find it:** best in full sun, moist soil, but will survive in part shade
**Edible parts:** leaves

### THE DETAILS

Beginning gardeners fall for chameleon plant because its foliage is gorgeous and it fills in fast. Its vigor is endearing at first, but after a year or two (when the chameleon plant has spread beyond its intended bounds), you may regret planting it. If, however, you can use chameleon plant appropriately, it's worth growing. I've seen it light up a hell strip (that hot, dry, untended strip of land between the sidewalk and the street) in Kentucky where it got no attention but did get good moisture. In dry gardens, it behaves itself demurely. It can also be used in water gardens, kept in containers. Leaves are vaguely heart-shaped and have dramatic variegation with creamy yellow and pinkish red patterns. The plant also produces small white flowers late in summer. Variegation is most intense in full sun.

Just two leaves of chameleon plant will liven up an entire salad.

### HOW TO HARVEST

Pinch or cut off the top leaves of chameleon plant to use as an herb in cooking or in salads. This is a strong-tasting leaf, so you won't need much. Try a bite straight off the plant before planning your menu, to give yourself a feel for how much you'll need. One warning: dried chameleon plant leaves have almost no flavor whatsoever, so use this herb fresh. There's no need to worry about overharvesting chameleon plant. If you're trying to control an out-of-bounds patch, yank it up by the roots and save a few leaves for dinner.

### HOW TO EAT IT

In Vietnamese cooking, an all-green variety of chameleon plant is called fish mint. It's used with grilled meat and fish, in spring rolls, and on top of noodle dishes. The leaves are minced or cut into small strips, because of their strong flavor.

The foliage of ornamental chameleon plant doesn't taste the slightest bit fishy to me. I find the taste to be tangy with vague undertones of ginger and a spiciness I can't describe. It's a unique flavor; you either love it or you hate it. (I love it.) A chiffonade of chameleon plant leaves adds both visual interest and a lively sour note to salads. You may use it in soups, cooked with the broth or served separately at the table so people can sprinkle on their own. Or mash the leaves into a paste to stir into broths, sauces, or wet rubs. It combines well with other strong herbs and spices like garlic, pepper, and basil.

> **The foliage of ornamental chameleon plant is tangy with vague undertones of ginger and a spiciness I can't describe.**

Chameleon plant will soon swallow this garden path.

SPRING    SUMMER    FALL    WINTER

# CHICKWEED

*Stellaria media*

**What it is:** a cool-weather annual weed
**Where to find it:** gardens, yards, roadsides; sun or shade
**Edible parts:** leaves and stems

The tender tips of chickweed include edible flowers.

## THE DETAILS

Chickweed is an annual with an unusual growing calendar. Seeds germinate in fall, and the leaves may overwinter, even under light snow. If the leaves die back, they'll regrow in spring, producing seed and dying off in the heat of summer. The seeds germinate a few months later in the cool weather, and the cycle begins again. Chickweed is one of the first greens to appear in spring, and it lasts longer than most in fall. I've even harvested it in winter, when the snow melts. It's tastiest in these cool seasons.

## HOW TO HARVEST

Chickweed grows juicy and thick in shade to part shade. In full sun the leaves will be smaller and perhaps less succulent. As the heat of summer arrives, the foliage becomes tough and slightly bitter.

Cut or pinch the ends of stems, gathering the last few inches to use raw. These youngest tips are the most tender parts of the plant. Or, if you're pulling up whole plants in a weeding frenzy, cut up the leaves and stems to use in cooking. Cooking greatly reduces the volume of chickweed, so harvest accordingly.

## HOW TO EAT IT

Chickweed is one of my favorite salad greens; it's mild and has good texture. It's crunchy and fresh in sandwiches and is an excellent substitute for sprouts or shredded lettuce. Chickweed can be substituted for basil or cilantro to create a creamy, mild version of pesto or chimichurri. Leaves soften up *very* quickly in cooking, so if you use it with other greens, add it at the end of the preparation. In egg dishes or pies, you don't need to cook chickweed before adding it to your dish. Fold the raw chopped greens into the mixture, then bake.

Look for lush mats of chickweed in moist, shady spots.

SPRING   SUMMER   FALL   WINTER

# GARLIC MUSTARD

## *Alliaria petiolata*

**What it is:** invasive plant, universally despised by conservationists
**Where to find it:** Where *not* to find it? It's everywhere: roadsides, woods, parks, your backyard. Garlic mustard prefers a little shade and moist soil but will also grow in less hospitable conditions.
**Edible parts:** leaves and young flower stalks

### THE DETAILS

There are entire websites devoted to the eradication of garlic mustard. This biennial, highly invasive plant produces seed that remains viable for up to five years, making it especially difficult to get rid of. It also has an allelopathic effect on surrounding soil, which helps muscle out competitors. Allelopathy is the production of chemical compounds (by plants) that suppress the germination or growth of neighboring, competing plants and reduce the populations of mycorrhizal fungi that help plants grow. As a result, garlic mustard crowds out a lot of less aggressive plants, reducing woodland diversity.

### HOW TO HARVEST

Although you'll only want to eat the tender young leaves of garlic mustard, go ahead and yank the plant out by the root, if you can. As with many tenacious weeds, a piece of root left behind will produce a new plant, so grab the garlic mustard firmly at ground level, then twist and pull. Garlic mustard has a taproot and won't give up its ground without a fight.

First-year foliage grows in a rosette; individual leaves are heart or kidney shaped, with toothed margins. Second-year leaves are elongated, and the plant produces a flower stalk with white four-petaled flowers in

Fresh, tasty leaves of garlic mustard are a vibrant green in early spring.

early summer. For culinary purposes, pick the leaves of first-year plants in early spring; pick the flower stalks before the flowers have opened. This will give you the most tender vegetables with the best garlic flavor.

In its second year, garlic mustard is easily identified by its white flowers. At this stage, though, the foliage and stems are too bitter to eat.

## HOW TO EAT IT

The first time I ate garlic mustard, I simply stuffed a few leaves into a rather bland cheese sandwich that I'd brought to work for lunch. My refrigerator was bare that morning, but the garlic mustard livened up my sandwich and made an impression. Add raw leaves to sandwiches and salads, but taste one first. The garlic taste is strong, especially in spring.

Garlic mustard pesto is a forager's classic. Since the leaves taste like garlic and are green, it takes the place of both garlic and basil in pesto. Add olive oil, salt and pepper, and your nut of choice. Since garlic mustard is a strong-flavored green, it combines well with milder greens in pita (see recipe on page 221) and soups, and also makes an excellent pasta stuffing. It's delicious in egg dishes like quiches, omelettes, and frittatas.

If you find second-year plants before they flower, once again, pull up the entire plant and save the flower stem. Snap off the bottoms of the stalks, as you would with asparagus, then remove the lower leaves, leaving only a few at the top. The stalks can be steamed or sautéed until tender, or chopped and added to stews and soups.

This plant is insanely nutritious, higher in fiber, beta-carotene, vitamins C and E, and zinc than either spinach or kale. It's also very high in calcium, iron, and omega-3 fatty acids.

# HOSTA

## *Hosta* species

**What it is:** ubiquitous foliage plant and favored deer snack
**Where to find it:** every home landscape and shade garden in America
**Edible parts:** early shoots and flowers

## THE DETAILS

Hostas are one of the world's most popular shade plants. There are so many different species and cultivars that it's

This little hosta shoot is at the perfect stage for harvesting.

possible to have a garden of nothing but hostas: blue leaves, chartreuse leaves, green margins and a white center, white margins with a green center, plants that are 3 feet tall, plants that are 3 inches tall . . . you get the picture. Deer love them, slugs love them, and why not? They're delicious.

## HOW TO HARVEST

To preserve the integrity of the plant, harvest from the perimeter, working your way evenly around the shape of the hosta. Don't remove more than one-third of the shoots. Or, if it's time to divide those giant hostas threatening to take over your garden, why not set aside part of the plant to serve for dinner?

The taste varies among species and cultivars, but

all are safe to eat. You'll have to experiment and see which you like best. The flowers are edible, too. Toss them in salads, or use them as a garnish; the blooms of *Hosta plantaginea* are especially fine.

## HOW TO EAT IT

Snails don't discriminate between tender young leaves and more fibrous, mature foliage, but humans should. Older leaves can be boiled for 15 to 20 minutes, then chopped and sautéed like other greens in soups or baked in a quiche or pie. To enjoy the taste of hosta in its prime, pick the young stems before the leaves completely unfurl.

The newest, tightest shoots can be chopped, stir-fried, and served over pasta or rice. (I'm not saying they taste like asparagus, but you can treat them like asparagus.) Slightly older but still tender shoots with the leaves just starting to open up can be briefly blanched, then sautéed and served as a vegetable with or without sauce. (Garlic, anyone? Perhaps a little soy?) The taste is light, mild, and fresh, somewhere between lettuce and young spinach. Stems maintain a pleasant crunch while the leaves become soft and creamy.

Feeling ambitious? In Japan, young hosta shoots are served as a vegetable dish called urui. Petioles (leaf stems) of *Hosta sieboldii* are skinned and parboiled, then chopped and served over rice. In northern Japan, *H. montana* has become a commercial crop. Plants are grown in greenhouses and kept covered to blanch and tenderize the foliage. What's for dinner? Boiled hosta with miso mustard sauce, of course.

All hostas are safe to eat, but the taste varies, so try a nibble here and there to see which one you like best.

# JAPANESE KNOTWEED

## *Fallopia japonica,* a.k.a. *Polygonum cuspidatum*

**What it is:** an aggressive weed or a garden perennial, depending on the cultivar and your point of view
**Where to find it:** gardens, roadsides, riverbanks
**Edible parts:** young stems

## THE DETAILS

Japanese knotweed grows in sun or shade, in roadside ditches, on steep embankments, in wet soils, and in city parks. Introduced to Victorian England as an ornamental plant, it became popular and spread to the United States, where in the 1970s and, '80s it was touted as a quick-growing plant, useful for stabilizing eroding roadsides and creating windbreaks and living fences. Too late, environmentalists realized that this aggressive plant was difficult to control. In the United Kingdom, it's now illegal to plant knotweed anywhere, and parts of the United States are following suit. Knotweed produces thousands of seeds per plant, and it also spreads by underground stolons.

In Darwinian terms, it's a very fit plant. Ornamental cultivars (*F. japonica* 'Variagata') are less aggressive, but if one is growing in your yard, you'll still want to keep an eye on it.

## HOW TO HARVEST

As Japanese knotweed matures, it gets tough and fibrous and requires peeling. Why make extra work for yourself? Harvest when the stalks are young and tender.

**EASY I.D.**
Knotweed is a perennial, so look for last year's tall dried stems to identify fresh new shoots in the spring. They'll poke up from the bases of the old brown stems.

Choose unbranched spears, between 8 and 16 inches tall. They may be as thick as your thumb or as slim as a pencil. Yank them up by the roots if you're on a crusade, or snap them off at ground level for an easier harvest. In less than half an hour you can easily pick 5 or 6 pounds of knotweed, enough for a batch of wine, some soup, and a couple of stir-fries.

## HOW TO EAT IT

There are so many things you can make with knotweed, you'll have no trouble using as much as you harvest. It keeps for months in the freezer, without blanching. Knotweed wine is one of my favorite homebrews; it takes less time to finish fermenting than many other wines and has a rich, tawny color. Knotweed can be substituted for rhubarb in pies, jams, and jellies; it combines well with strawberries, blueberries, and apples. Or you can use knotweed as a vegetable; it's tart and crunchy in stir-fries and lemony delicious under hollandaise. My favorite way to eat knotweed: knotweed soup. It's creamalicious. Besides, eating it turns lunch into environmental activism.

It's also good for you. Knotweed contains large amounts of resveratrol, a chemical compound that some scientists believe has beneficial effects as an antioxidant. Active research is ongoing to confirm claims that resveratrol lowers blood sugar and slows the aging process, but no peer-reviewed scientific studies have been published to date. Most commercial resveratrol supplements are made from Japanese knotweed.

Japanese knotweed is often found along roadsides, woodland edges, and riverbanks.

SPRING   SUMMER   FALL   WINTER

# JOSEPH'S COAT, CHINESE SPINACH

*Amaranthus tricolor*

**What it is:** a colorful annual
**Where to find it:** sunny gardens
**Edible parts:** leaves and seeds

### THE DETAILS

In Southeast Asia, Joseph's coat is a popular leaf vegetable. In India the young stems are served as a side dish. In eastern and southern Africa the plant is often found in family vegetable gardens. Yet most Western cultures consider this an exclusively ornamental plant. Modern cultivars have been hybridized for flashy variegated foliage but are just as nutritious as their more modest vegetable cousins. This showy garden annual grows best in full sun and rich, well-drained soil. It doesn't transplant well; you're better off growing this plant from seed.

> The leaves of Joseph's coat can be eaten raw in salads, where their vibrant colors liven up a bowl of greens.

### HOW TO HARVEST

Pinch or snip stems just above a node to accomplish two tasks at once: pruning your plants to make them bushier and collecting greens for the supper table. Other amaranths (*A. caudatus*, for one; also known as "love lies bleeding," it's another fantastically gorgeous garden annual) are cultivated for their seeds, which are produced in copious amounts and can be used as a gluten-free grain substitute.

### HOW TO EAT IT

The leaves of Joseph's coat can be eaten raw in salads, where their vibrant colors liven up a bowl of greens. It is also an excellent spinach substitute, especially in hot weather when spinach languishes and amaranths are just hitting their stride. It can be steamed, sautéed, or stir-fried, and like spinach, it reduces in volume when cooked.

Not surprisingly, this mild green is often prepared with strong spices. Many Indian recipes combine the leaves and stems with curry, chiles, and cumin. In Chinese and Vietnamese cooking it's often prepared with onions and garlic. It can also be finely chopped and added to meatballs or meatloaf, where its texture and color are a welcome surprise.

Joseph's coat epitomizes the idea of ornamental edible: so pretty, so tasty.

SPRING    SUMMER    FALL    WINTER

# MALABAR SPINACH

*Basella alba*

**What it is:** a tropical vine used as an annual in temperate climates
**Where to find it:** gardens
**Edible parts:** leaves and stems

## THE DETAILS

Malabar spinach (no relation to true spinach) has been a popular ornamental vine for years. It grows quickly, covering a tripod or trellis in a single season. The leaves are dark green, strongly textured, and glossy, making it an excellent backdrop for flowering annuals in containers and in the ground. The stems of some forms (the cultivar 'Rubra', for example) are an ornamental red color. Plants produce small white flowers that are followed by dark purple seeds. The leaves and stems of Malabar spinach are edible and highly mucilaginous. They are used frequently in Africa and in several cuisines of the South Pacific, including India, Vietnam, and the Philippines.

## HOW TO HARVEST

Malabar spinach grows very quickly in the high heat of summer, so you should be able to harvest regularly. Because the leaves are so mucilaginous, choose the smallest, most tender leaves to eat raw; these contain the least mucilage. If you plan to cook your Malabar spinach, you should be able to harvest a meal every few weeks. To preserve the beauty of your plant, prune the vines just above a node. Malabar spinach cooks down in volume, although not as much as true spinach.

## HOW TO EAT IT

Raw leaves make a mild salad green. But there's so much more you can do with this versatile and sturdy plant. And since it thrives in the heat of summer, when spinach most definitely does not, make it your go-to green in July and August. Use the leaves in egg dishes and stir-fries, the way you would spinach. Dice the succulent stems, sauté them, and add them to stews, soups, or the sauce of your choice.

Look to Malabar spinach's geographic area of origin for inspiration, and spice it with curry, ginger, cardamom, garlic, chiles, cumin, or onions. It stands alone as a substantial vegetable dish or combines well with pasta, chickpeas, rice, and other grains.

> Since Malabar spinach thrives in the heat of summer, when spinach most definitely does not, make it your go-to green in July and August.

These glossy Malabar spinach leaves are at the perfect stage for harvesting.

SPRING   SUMMER   FALL   WINTER

# MINER'S LETTUCE

## *Claytonia perfoliata,* a.k.a. *Montia perfoliata*

**What it is:** a succulent, rampant ground cover with attractive round leaves
**Where to find it:** common along the Pacific Northwest coast, rare in other places; requires moist soil
**Edible parts:** leaves

## THE DETAILS

Yet another roadside weed, miner's lettuce got its name during the gold rush when fresh vegetables were hard to come by. It was a plentiful and excellent salad green, and its high vitamin C levels kept scurvy at bay.

Succulent and crunchy, miner's lettuce stays sweet and mild even after it flowers, unlike many greens. Most miner's lettuce is easily recognizable by the round leaf, perforated at its center by the stem. However, depending on the location or time of year, the terminal leaves may be pointier or more wing-shaped. Small pink or white flowers are held above the disc-shaped leaf in spring and are also edible. In full sun, miner's

In just a few minutes you can gather a salad's worth of miner's lettuce.

lettuce will die back in summer. In shady, moist conditions, it remains lush and edible. It often grows in great abundance.

## HOW TO HARVEST

Pinch the round leaf off the plant, leaving behind the long, slim basal leaves. It's okay if a little bit of stem comes along, and the flowers are also edible.

Plants growing in shade will be tastier than those growing in sun. Drought stresses plants and gives foliage a reddish tint. These leaves may develop a bitter taste, so focus on picking green leaves from shady, moist places.

Although it is classified as an annual plant, there are some people who swear it's a perennial.

In any case, miner's lettuce self-seeds freely and returns to the same spot year after year. In many places it's one of the earliest spring greens to appear, and in mild climates it stays green throughout the winter months. If you're growing a crop of miner's lettuce on the East Coast, you'll need to order seeds to start, but you should only have to plant it once.

## HOW TO EAT IT

Miner's lettuce is such a mild, tasty leaf, it's best appreciated fresh and raw, in either a salad or a sandwich. It's one of the few greens you could make an entire salad out of and find it neither boring nor overpowering. It needs nothing more than a simple vinaigrette and a few crumbles of goat cheese. If you must cook it, please don't overdo it. A quick steam or brief stir-fry (2 to 3 minutes) will keep it crisp.

Succulent and crunchy, miner's lettuce is a refreshing, mild green.

# NASTURTIUM

## *Tropaeolum majus*

**What it is:** an annual garden flower
**Where to find it:** sun to part sun; gardens
**Edible parts:** leaves and flowers

### THE DETAILS

This familiar garden annual grows easily from seed, and its flowers come in many colors. It quickly reaches blooming size and performs well as a ground cover in sunny gardens or as a spiller in containers and hanging baskets.

### HOW TO HARVEST

Flowers should be picked when young and fresh. Small, young leaves may be harvested to use raw, and larger leaves can be picked and blanched. Nasturtium flowers and leaves can be harvested at any time during the growing season; they don't get bitter in high temperatures. Be sure to pick both the stem and the leaf when harvesting. You won't eat the stem, but it looks sad to leave a naked stem standing there, shorn of its leaf. Seedpods are often harvested, pickled, and used as caper substitutes. Since I don't like capers, I'd rather leave the pods on the plants to ripen and produce seed for next year.

### HOW TO EAT IT

Nasturtium blooms make a more interesting garnish than most flowers; they have a distinctive peppery-horseradishy taste, not too strong but not shy and retiring either. They can also be added to salads, floated on cold soups, or sprinkled on top of rice dishes. Tender leaves can be eaten raw in salads or sandwiches; their flavor is slightly stronger than that of the flowers. Raw leaves and/or flowers can also be used to make a peppery pesto.

> The most interesting way to use nasturtium leaves is to blanch and stuff them. Older leaves may grow to 4 to 6 inches in diameter, providing wrappers suitable for stuffing.

The most interesting way to use nasturtium leaves is to blanch and stuff them. Older leaves may grow to 4 to 6 inches in diameter, providing wrappers suitable for stuffing. Blanch them in boiling water for a minute to render them pliable. Place a teaspoon of softened goat cheese in the center of the leaf, then roll it, turning the ends under and tucking them in to create a neat little package. The peppery taste of the leaf complements the goat cheese perfectly. Nasturtium leaves are not as coarse as grape or cabbage leaves and won't stand up to prolonged cooking times.

The foliage and flowers of nasturtium have a distinctive peppery taste.

SPRING  SUMMER  FALL  WINTER

# OSTRICH FERN

## *Matteuccia struthiopteris* and *M. pensylvanica*

**What it is:** a stately perennial fern
**Where to find it:** woods, shade gardens
**Edible parts:** fiddleheads (early, furled leaves)

### THE DETAILS

While most fern fronds emerge as fiddleheads, not all fiddleheads are equally tasty. In fact, some are downright bitter and should be avoided. The young foliage of ostrich fern is considered to be one of the most delicious, and the plant is a beloved component of traditional shade gardens. Ostrich ferns have papery sheaths covering the emerging fiddleheads and an obvious deep groove along the inside of a smooth stem. The sheaths are easily removed, unlike the stubborn, wooly coverings of cinnamon fern (*Osmunda cinnamomea*). These important identifying characteristics (groove, papery sheath) will keep you from making an unpleasant (but not deadly) culinary error.

### HOW TO HARVEST

When picking fiddleheads, distribute your harvest carefully. Don't take more than two or three fronds from any one plant. This leaves the plant with enough foliage to persist. Also, only pick fronds that are still tightly furled. Unfurled fronds are tough and unpalatable at best; some people consider them toxic. Either way, they're not good eats. You may,

Soft, plumy fronds are too mature to eat but still lovely in the garden.

These fiddleheads are at the perfect stage for harvesting.

Fresh fiddleheads, harvested at their peak, have a flavor that's somewhere between green beans and asparagus.

however, include about 6 inches of straight stem in your harvest. The season for ostrich fern fiddleheads is all too brief: two or three weeks at best. Ostrich ferns produce two distinct types of fronds: sterile, deciduous, plumy green fronds emerge in early spring, and fertile, stiff, dark brown, persistent ferns emerge in fall. Fertile fronds are not edible.

Ostrich fern is easy to find in nurseries and garden centers. Since the plant has become endangered in some areas (due to nonsustainable wild harvesting), why not plant a border in a shady section of your garden and reap the benefits, both visual and culinary?

## HOW TO EAT IT

While some people eat the youngest, freshest, most tightly furled fiddleheads raw, others cannot tolerate the plant as a raw vegetable. To be on the safe side, boil your fiddleheads for 10 minutes.

As a traditional and treasured spring vegetable in New England and eastern Canada, fiddleheads are grocery store fare and are sold canned or fresh. You can freeze or can your own fiddleheads if you have an abundant crop. Be sure to boil them for 10 minutes first.

Add boiled fiddleheads to pasta with a little butter and a grating of parmesan cheese. The taste is somewhere between green bean and asparagus. They make an excellent stand-alone vegetable when topped with soy sauce or lemon juice. And if you're feeling really indulgent, boiled fiddleheads, lightly sautéed with garlic, make a delicious topping for a goat cheese tart.

## EASY I.D.

Ostrich fern forms a perennial crown that gets bigger every year. New crowns emerge from underground rhizomes. The deep V groove and papery covering are two key features for easy identification.

SPRING   SUMMER   FALL   WINTER

# OXEYE DAISY, MARGUERITE DAISY

*Leucanthemum vulgare,* a.k.a. *Chrysanthemum leucanthemum*

**What it is:** an old-fashioned perennial flower
**Where to find it:** yards, fields, roadsides
**Edible parts:** leaves, flower petals (ray flowers)

## THE DETAILS

Related to florist's chrysanthemum, this familiar daisy spreads easily. It grows best in full sun but tolerates part shade, although it will produce fewer flowers in lower light. Oxeye daisy grows primarily as a basal rosette of glossy, deep green foliage with scalloped margins. In early summer the plant produces one or more flowering stems. Basal leaves are larger and juicier than the stem leaves, and the basal rosette overwinters in milder climates.

> Leaves of oxeye daisy are stronger than mild greens such as miner's lettuce and bishop's weed; the flavor is an interesting combination of spinach, lemon, and pepper.

## HOW TO HARVEST

The composite flower of oxeye daisies is actually made up of sterile ray flowers (what we consider the petals) and fertile disc flowers (what we consider the center). White flower petals should be plucked as soon as the blooms have fully opened. Whole flowers can be used as garnish, but the orange-yellow disc flowers may contain insects attracted to their pollen, so be sure to wash them thoroughly before adding them to your plate.

Individual leaves may be plucked from basal rosettes. Since the plant is often found in abundance, spread your harvest among several plants. This allows you to pick plenty of leaves to eat, and leave enough foliage behind for the plants to survive. A few states have classified the oxeye daisy as a noxious weed and forbidden commercial sales. Perhaps the best way to rid yourself of unwanted oxeye daisies is to harvest the entire plant and use the foliage in salads. The root system is relatively shallow, making this plant easier to pull up than other edible weeds like dandelion or bishop's weed.

## HOW TO EAT IT

Oxeye daisy flowers are attractive, but their flavor isn't especially remarkable. It's a fresh, mild taste, and the bloom is pretty on a plate as an edible garnish.

The leaves, however, are an interesting, tasty green. Nibble a leaf before picking, to be sure you like the flavor. It's stronger than mild greens such as miner's lettuce and bishop's weed; the flavor is an interesting combination of spinach, lemon, and pepper. Raw, it's snappy tucked into sandwiches and mixed with other greens in salads. Cooked oxeye daisy foliage mixes well with other greens in pies, soups, and stews, or in quesadillas. Leaves are tastiest when picked before the plant blooms.

Oxeye daisies have foliage to spare! Harvest a few leaves from several plants, and you'll never notice the missing foliage.

SPRING  SUMMER  FALL  WINTER

# PINEAPPLE WEED

## *Matricaria matricarioides*

**What it is:** a tough, resilient, native North American perennial weed
**Where to find it:** poor soils, full sun, roadsides, fields, playgrounds, yards
**Edible parts:** flowers

> Related to chamomile, pineapple weed has an enticing scent and a history of use as a sleep aid.

### THE DETAILS

Nobody plants pineapple weed. I've never seen seeds for sale. But it's a welcome sight and smell wherever it crops up, and it crops up everywhere. It grows north of the Arctic Circle all the way down to southern California, and across the entire country. Pineapple weed spreads moderately on the edges of lawns and in neglected spaces. It's not bad to look at either, with finely cut leaves and

Both the flowers and foliage of pineapple weed smell great, but the flowers are tastier.

## EASY I.D.

The easiest way to identify the plant is to crush a flower between your fingers. If you don't immediately smell the sweet scent of pineapple, you've got the wrong plant!

## HOW TO EAT IT

The most popular use for pineapple weed is as a tea. Use either dried or fresh flowers to make an infusion, but if you're using fresh flowers, you'll need twice as many. Fresh herbs can be 80 to 90 percent water; drying concentrates the flavor. Since taste-producing volatile oils evaporate over time, try to use dried herbs within 6 to 12 months. Pineapple weed flowers have a natural sweetness, but I still think the tea benefits from a drop of honey. It's tasty hot or iced.

Toss the fresh flowers into a salad and watch the faces of your guests when they bite into an unexpected burst of pineappley goodness. Or mix fresh flowers into chicken salad for a sweet, fruity flavor. How about sprinkling them on top of cold sesame noodles? This plant won't make a meal, but it adds an interesting, unexpected accent to any number of dishes.

prolific, small yellow-green flowers. Related to chamomile, pineapple weed has an enticing scent and a history of use as a sleep aid.

## HOW TO HARVEST

Gently pull the flowers off their stems, leaving the plants behind to produce another round. Pineapple weed blooms reliably all summer long. Flowers are plentiful on each plant; you should be able to harvest enough for immediate use and for drying some to store for future use. While the foliage is perfectly safe to eat, it lacks the delicious scent and taste of the flowers. If a few leaves get mixed in with your flower harvest, don't worry, but focus on picking the blooms.

SPRING SUMMER FALL WINTER

# PURSLANE

## *Portulaca oleracea*

**What it is:** a succulent, common annual weed
**Where to find it:** sidewalks, roadsides, gardens, in full sun and dry conditions
**Edible parts:** leaves and stems

## THE DETAILS

Next time you're in Whole Foods check the produce section and chances are you'll find purslane. Yes, the *exact same* purslane growing through the cracks in the sidewalk outside your house, only cleaned up and with a hefty price tag. It's high in iron, vitamins A and C, and omega-3 fatty acids. In many countries it's cultivated as a food plant,

Thick stems make this portulaca perfect for stir-frying.

yet here we pull it up as a weed. This isn't an aggressive plant. It grows rapidly but doesn't muscle out other plants. Purslane reseeds readily; you may want to remove seedlings (and eat them!) before they get established.

## HOW TO HARVEST

If you're cultivating a purslane patch at home, pinch off the top leaves. This delivers a modest crop and encourages branching, which ensures future harvests throughout the season. These youngest leaves are excellent raw: tender and juicy. At the end of the season, or if you're weeding, pull up the entire plant and use it as a cooked or pickled vegetable.

## HOW TO EAT IT

Raw purslane is crunchy and slightly tart. It's great in a salad or sandwich. To use raw, pinch the leaves in pairs, focusing on the youngest, most tender greens. Purslane has traditionally been pickled in a brine similar to cucumber pickles, and if you have

These young leaves are tender enough to enjoy raw.

tons of purslane, go ahead and make pickles. Older, thicker stems make more substantial pickles. I prefer to focus on the pure purslane taste.

Cooked purslane tastes something like spinach, but the texture is quite different and it doesn't reduce in volume like spinach does. It is slightly mucilaginous, but seriously, nothing like okra. Purslane works well in stir-fries, egg dishes, and casseroles. In soups and stews it adds substance. My favorite: sauté with olive oil, feta, garlic, oregano, and a few tomatoes for a delicious Mediterranean side dish.

> The youngest leaves are excellent raw: tender and juicy, crunchy and slightly tart.

SPRING SUMMER FALL WINTER

# SHEEP SORREL

*Rumex acetosella*

**What it is:** a perennial lawn weed
**Where to find it:** lawns, fields, roadsides; moister soils produce larger, lusher leaves
**Edible parts:** leaves

## THE DETAILS

You could have sheep sorrel growing all over your yard and not even know it. A low-growing, mild-mannered weed, its light green, arrow-shaped leaves don't jump out at you, although they're easily recognizable once you're familiar with them. A close relative of the French sorrel sold in supermarkets, sheep sorrel is equally tangy but has smaller leaves. The sour taste of sheep sorrel comes from oxalic acid, which is toxic in giant doses. Giant. Doses. There are no confirmed cases of human poisoning from consuming sheep sorrel.

## HOW TO HARVEST

Sheep sorrel foliage stays tasty all season long. During times of drought, leaves will be smaller and may take on a reddish tint, but they are still edible. Plants growing in part shade and moist soils will produce larger, lusher leaves, making it faster to amass a sizable harvest. Pick leaves at will. Sheep sorrel spreads by underground rhizomes as well as by seed. You'd be hard pressed to make a dent in the plant population.

## HOW TO EAT IT

Sheep sorrel leaves are delicious and lemony. Raw, they make an excellent addition to any salad or sandwich, livening up milder greens. Add them to potato salad to give it a zing. Cooked, they're a tangy element in vegetable dishes and a key component in sorrel soup. Purée the boiled or sautéed leaves to make a lemony sauce for chicken and fish. Leaves reduce considerably in volume when cooked, so pick three or four times as much as you think you need.

> A close relative of the French sorrel sold in supermarkets, sheep sorrel is equally tangy but has smaller leaves.

These small sorrel leaves pack a tangy punch.

SPRING  SUMMER  FALL  WINTER

# SPIDERWORT

*Tradescantia virginiana*

**What it is:** a perennial with flowers in blue, white, or magenta
**Where to find it:** gardens; full sun to part shade
**Edible parts:** young shoots, flowers, and leaves

## THE DETAILS

This popular garden plant is best known for its saturated, vibrant, purple-blue flowers in early summer. It grows best in sun to part sun. Each succulent stem produces several small flowers, each lasting only one day. Plants bloom over several weeks and grow well in containers.

## HOW TO HARVEST

Flowers can be used raw as an edible garnish, but the leaves and stems are best when cooked. Both can be harvested at any time during the growing season. Since they flower in early summer, why not wait until after they finish blooming before you cut them for cooking? The stems get very floppy after flowering. By cutting them

Young spiderwort shoots are tasty, but if you harvest now, you'll miss the flowers.

> Flowers can be used raw as an edible garnish, but the leaves and stems are best when cooked. Both can be harvested at any time during the growing season.

back to soil level, you not only get an edible harvest but may also produce a new round of blooms.

## HOW TO EAT IT

Spiderwort stems are highly mucilaginous when raw, but cooking removes the slimy quality and lets you focus on their mild, green taste. The leaves make a tasty addition to eggs, soups, pasta, or rice. The stems have enough substance and flavor to stand alone as a vegetable — chopped, sautéed, and tossed with soy sauce. You can also add them to quiches and casseroles, where they maintain their texture, unlike other leafy greens.

After flowering has finished, cut back the floppy stems and eat them.

SPRING  SUMMER  FALL  WINTER

# SPRUCE

## *Picea* species

**What it is:** an evergreen tree
**Where to find it:** gardens, parks, yards
**Edible parts:** young tips of branches

## THE DETAILS

Spruce trees come in many shapes and sizes, and all of them produce edible tips. These popular evergreens grow best in full sun locations, although they'll tolerate a few hours of shade. History books tell of explorers staving off scurvy by drinking a tea made from spruce needles, but most people don't consider this anything more than famine food.

Douglas fir (*Pseudotsuga menziesii*) and our native hemlock (*Tsuga canadensis*) also produce tasty shoots.

## HOW TO HARVEST

In early spring, the tips of spruce branches produce feathery new growth, initially covered in brown, papery sheaths. When the sheaths begin to fall off, snip the new growth. The dividing line between old and new growth is clear both visually and texturally. Where old growth is dark green, hard, and pointy, new growth is light green, soft, and flexible. As the growing season progresses, these new tips will expand, darken, and harden. I don't recommend using older tips for cooking. Although they are still high in vitamin C, their taste is intensely resinous. Since you are removing the current

### LOOK-ALIKE TO AVOID

Yews (left) are evergreens that produce soft red fruit. Their poisonous, flat, dark green needles are arranged in pairs along opposite sides of the stem and should NOT be used for any kind of cooking!

Look for the soft, light green tips of spruce to harvest.

year's growth, spread your harvest around the circumference of the tree to avoid a lopsided look. In subsequent years, harvest from a different set of branches.

## HOW TO EAT IT

This is not a common taste for most of us, but it's refreshing and exciting to people with an open and adventurous palate. Once you understand the taste, you'll be able to combine it freely with fish and meat, soups and stews. It's extremely versatile and complements both sweet and savory dishes. To make spruce salt or spruce sugar, add equal parts salt or sugar and spruce tips to the bowl of a food processor, then pulse until the mix is finely chopped. Spread it out on a cookie sheet and allow it to dry at room temperature, then store in a jar.

Spruce tips boiled in a simple syrup make a refreshing jelly or sorbet. (Strain the spruce and discard.) Or stuff a quart jar with spruce tips and pour vodka to fill the jar. Store the jar in a dark place for a week, then strain the vodka off the spruce. To make an exciting mixed drink, coat the rim of a martini glass with spruce sugar, combine the chilled vodka with a sploosh of elderflower soda, then garnish with a whole spruce tip. It's a fantasy woodland cocktail.

The gorgeous foliage of blue spruce is delicious when harvested at the soft and tender stage.

SPRING    SUMMER    FALL    WINTER

# STONECROP, ORPINE

## *Sedum, Hylotelephium, Rhodiola* species

**What they are:** drought-tolerant perennials with attractive flowers
**Where to find them:** sunny gardens
**Edible parts:** leaves

### THE DETAILS

These succulent garden plants thrive in dry soils and require little maintenance. They grow best in full sun but will tolerate some shade, although they'll produce fewer flowers with less light. The upright species, including *Sedum* 'Autum Joy', bloom in late summer to early fall and provide excellent winter interest when their dried flowers are left to catch a sprinkling of snow.

The taste varies from species to species, as well as seasonally, but generally the foliage is juicy and has a tart, peppery taste. One species, common stonecrop (*Sedum acre*), has a *very* strong-tasting leaf and should be chopped and used as a seasoning rather than eaten whole.

Harvesting a few leaves from these regal sedums won't detract from their beauty.

> The taste varies from species to species, as well as seasonally, but generally the foliage is juicy and has a tart, peppery taste.

The genus *Sedum* has recently been reorganized, and several plants have been moved into different genera. There is some controversy over the names, so you may still find them labeled as sedums in garden centers.

## HOW TO HARVEST

Taste a leaf before you harvest to make sure you like it. A leaf in midsummer may be unpleasantly bitter, but in fall a leaf from that same plant will be juicy and barely tart. Plants growing in shade may be tasty all season long, but plants in full sun are best harvested in spring or fall. Pick the youngest leaves, spreading your harvest around so as not to denude any one stem.

Dainty rosettes of early sedum foliage are especially tender.

## HOW TO EAT IT

Raw stonecrop foliage adds a juiciness and crunch to salads and sandwiches. Those with variegated leaves contribute visual interest. You might also nibble on a few leaves while doing your garden chores. Although leaves can be sautéed and served as a cooked vegetable — cooked leaves have a milder taste, so they combine well with stronger-tasting greens and vegetables — raw is really the way to go.

SPRING    SUMMER    FALL    WINTER

# SWEETFERN

*Comptonia peregrina*

**What it is:** not a fern! a small shrub with fragrant, narrow, scalloped, dark green foliage
**Where to find it:** mixed woods, roadsides in sun to dappled shade; sandy, poor soils
**Edible parts:** leaves

Its unusual leaf shape makes sweetfern easy to spot. Crush a leaf between your fingers to release its fragrance and confirm your identification.

## THE DETAILS

Sweetfern grows where many plants will not: in sandy soils with poor nutrition. Extremely cold hardy, sweetfern is happiest in USDA Hardiness Zones 2 to 6. Rumor has it that sweetfern is difficult to transplant, but I have not found this to be true. The problem is that most people's garden soil is too darn good, and a heavy clay soil is a death sentence. Keep it in full to part sun, a fast-draining soil, and don't fertilize it. With those conditions, sweetfern not only transplants easily but spreads nicely too. Its foliage is so fragrant that you don't even need to crush it to enjoy the scent. The heat of direct summer sun releases the unmistakable smell of sweetfern into the surrounding air.

> Sweetfern makes an excellent rub for meat and fish and can be used this way either fresh or dried.

## HOW TO HARVEST

Prune the tops off sweetfern branches, making the cut just above a node. Choose flexible, unblemished foliage, then strip the leaves off the branches and use either fresh or dry.

## HOW TO EAT IT

I have nothing against tea. I just don't consider it food, so when someone tells me a plant makes a great tea, I think, "Okay, but what else?" The most common use of sweetfern foliage is in tea, which can be made from either fresh or dried leaves. I don't deny it's a tasty beverage, hot or cold, and the taste is more distinctive and interesting than most herbal teas. But let's think outside the tea ball.

Sweetfern makes an excellent rub for meat and fish and can be used this way either fresh or dried. The foliage dries quickly. To dry it, use an elastic band to tie together several branches, then hang them somewhere out of direct sun; it shouldn't take more than a week to dry. In a dehydrator the leaves will finish in 1 to 2 hours. I prefer to use the foliage fresh when possible (during the growing season), but I also store dried leaves in my spice cupboard. Keep the leaves whole until you're ready to use them, then crumble or grind them with a mortar and pestle.

Fresh leaves can be finely chopped by hand or in a spice grinder. Sweetfern has a strong scent, but the taste is mild, green, and earthy. It combines well with spicebush berries and wild ginger.

SPRING    SUMMER    FALL    WINTER

# WINTERGREEN, TEABERRY

*Gaultheria procumbens*

**What it is:** an evergreen ground cover; technically, a (very) small shrub
**Where to find it:** in the woods, shade to part shade; acid soils
**Edible parts:** leaves and berries

## THE DETAILS

For anyone who knows Teaberry gum, the flavor of wintergreen will be pleasantly familiar. It's a subtle taste, more sophisticated than the outright pow of peppermint or spearmint. Nibble the ripe berries for a taste of wintergreen essence, but don't expect great texture. The fruit is dry and a little mealy. Wintergreen does best in acid soil and is a slow grower. Individual stems produce two to five glossy green leaves and one to three berries, on average.

## HOW TO HARVEST

Wintergreen spreads by underground stolons and is often found in large clumps. Because it is a modest plant, it's easy to overlook, especially when the forest floor is covered with hay-scented ferns

and lowbush blueberry. In fall, when the ferns die back, the small, shiny, elliptical green leaves are easier to spot. Plants in sunnier spots produce more berries than plants in shade.

Wintergreen leaves can be harvested any time of year. Snip a leaf or two from each plant, leaving at least one leaf on each stem so the plant can photosynthesize. As temperatures drop in fall, wintergreen foliage takes on a red tint. These leaves will impart some of their color to whatever you make with them. Bonus!

---

### WINTERGREEN WARNING

The characteristic taste of wintergreen comes from methyl salicylate, a chemical compound similar in structure to the active ingredient in aspirin. People with aspirin allergies should not consume wintergreen. Also, a quick look around the Internet produces numerous warnings about the toxicity of wintergreen oil. If this scares you, please don't eat wintergreen! But if you're curious (or skeptical), do a little more research. All the current studies are for consumption of pure, steam-distilled wintergreen oil, which is highly concentrated. There is no reason to believe that a cup of wintergreen tea or a serving of wintergreen ice cream will be dangerous for anyone who doesn't have a sensitivity to aspirin.

---

## HOW TO EAT IT

I don't get excited about teas in general, but it's worth mentioning that wintergreen was once such a popular tea plant that it was given the common name teaberry. I prefer to use it in ice cream and booze, both of which I find exponentially more interesting than tea. However you choose to use the foliage, it requires simple pre-treatment to fully release its characteristic flavor.

Fill a jar with leaves, then add water and allow the foliage to macerate (steep) at room temperature for three to five days. Taste the infusion periodically to monitor its strength. I suggest making an extra-strong brew that can then be diluted with additional water (for tea or sorbet) or with heavy cream (2 parts cream to 1 part teaberry water) for wintergreen ice cream. A jar filled with leaves and rum produces a delicious, warming winter aperitif.

> For anyone who knows Teaberry gum, the flavor of wintergreen will be pleasantly familiar.

Cold winter temperatures may give wintergreen leaves a reddish tint. Both red and green leaves are equally tasty.

# CHAPTER 4

## THE FRUITS OF NATURE'S LABOR:
# Edible Flowers and Fruits

Spicebush berries are both sweet and savory.

# It's amazing how many fruit trees people already grow . . .

but not for their fruit! Many of our favorite flowering trees (crab apples, hawthorns, mountain ash) do double or triple duty in the garden, providing flowers in spring, fruit in summer, and colorful foliage in autumn. So while you may have admired the white spring blooms and orange fall foliage of serviceberry, you may not have ever tasted its luscious purple berries in between.

Any flower that is successfully pollinated will produce a fruit, and if that fruit gets what it needs in terms of water, light, and nutrition, it should ripen to a plump maturity. Of course, if you harvest your edible flowers, you'll reduce your fruit crop, but it's entirely possible to drink your elderflower champagne and leave enough to ripen to produce a few pints of elderberry jelly in the fall. In this chapter you'll find fruits and edible flowers that don't require the careful pest control or pruning of traditional fruit crops but offer equally excellent eating.

SPRING  SUMMER  FALL  WINTER

# CHOKEBERRY

## *Aronia melanocarpa* and *A. arbutifolia*

**What it is:** a deciduous shrub
**Where to find it:** gardens, woods; full to part sun; moist soils
**Edible parts:** berries

## THE DETAILS

Chokeberries are medium-sized ornamental shrubs that grow best in sun. They're most beautiful in fall, when their foliage turns a vibrant red and their fruit ripens to either purple-black (*Aronia melanocarpa*) or red (*A. arbutifolia*). Spring flowers of both species are white and fragrant. Raw berries are quite astringent and not terrific for eating out of hand. Their juice, however, is tart and complex, and growing in popularity. It's high in vitamin C and antioxidants, and chokeberry is a well-known commercial crop in parts of Europe. It's also grown commercially in the United States, although the juice is usually blended with other fruit juices, then bottled. Some larger grocery stores (Trader Joe's, Whole Foods) have recently started to sell 100 percent aronia juice. Try a bottle, and if you like the taste, plant the shrub!

## HOW TO HARVEST

Unlike many berries, which are sweeter after being touched by a frost, chokeberries are juiciest and tastiest when they first ripen. Left on the branch they'll dry out, so you'll have to choose between beauty in the landscape and tastiness in the kitchen. Larger berries are usually best, and taste varies from shrub to shrub, so try a few berries from different plants before you harvest.

Please note, choke*berries* are not the same as choke-*cherries*. Chokecherries come from *Prunus virginiana,* a small tree. While this fruit is also purple-black (like that of *Aronia*

These red chokeberry (*Aronia arbutifolia*) fruits are ripe for the picking.

> Chokeberries are high in vitamin C and antioxidants, and are a well-known commercial crop in parts of Europe.

The fruit of black chokeberry (*Aronia melanocarpa*) ripens to a deep purple color.

*melanocarpa*), its growth habit and taste are quite different. It's an excellent wild edible, but not a tree that has great landscape value in the garden.

## HOW TO EAT IT

Raw chokeberries will make you pucker right up. Although some people do enjoy eating them straight off the branch, I'm not one of them. Juicing the fruit removes the sharpest edge of sourness and provides a juice that can be drunk plain or sweetened. If you don't have a juicer, put the berries in a large pot and add just enough water to cover the fruit. You can mash them raw, which produces a fresher-tasting juice but takes more elbow grease. Or bring the fruit and water to a boil to soften the fruit, then mash. Strain the juice through a jelly bag and taste, then sweeten if necessary.

You may love the juice so much that you drink it all, but chokeberry juice has many other uses. The tartness of the berry stands up to sugar, and its vibrant color makes it gorgeous in sorbets or ice cream. It's naturally high in pectin and makes a beautiful, richly colored tart jelly, without the addition of extra pectin. When reduced to a syrup with the addition of sugar, you'll have an unusual and colorful addition to white wine or prosecco. And if you've got a bumper crop, why not make a gallon of chokeberry wine?

Both species of chokeberry produce fragrant white flowers in spring.

# CORNELIAN CHERRY, CORNELS

*Cornus mas*

**What it is:** a small to medium-sized deciduous flowering tree or multi-stemmed shrub with an illustrious history
**Where to find it:** gardens, woods, parks
**Edible parts:** fruit

> Cornelian cherries make an excellent jam or fruit leather after the heated pulp is run through a food mill.

## THE DETAILS

The cornelian cherry isn't actually a cherry tree; it's a dogwood. Cornelian cherry produces numerous delicate yellow flowers in early spring. As a landscape tree, it's primarily planted for its bloom. As a harbinger of the season, it's a joyous sight. Fruit may be yellow or red, and each has a large seed, so it's not great for eating out of hand. In addition to ornamental flowers and

Cornelian cherry blooms in late winter or early spring, depending on where you live.

berries, it has red foliage in fall.

Did you know that the Trojan horse is said to have been built from the wood of the cornelian cherry? Its flexible wood was also used for spears in ancient Greece, and in *The Odyssey*, Circe feeds cornel fruit to Odysseus's men, whom she has turned into pigs. This is a tree with history.

## HOW TO HARVEST

Pick cornelian cherries when they darken and are soft to the touch. The colors of both red and yellow fruit will deepen with time; this deeper color signals ripeness. Trees are often highly floriferous, and the resulting fruit crop can be prolific, especially if the tree grows in full sun. In shade, trees may produce only a handful of berries.

## HOW TO EAT IT

This is a sour fruit. Try one raw to get a feel for it, but considering the large pit size and its extreme tartness, you probably won't want to eat a lot of them plain. Cornelian cherries make an excellent jam or fruit leather after the heated pulp is run through a food mill. I've read that some people chop the pits and leave them in for a little extra crunch. Those people must have giant teeth made of stone, because cornel seeds are large and very hard.

Strained juice can be used for jelly or syrup, and the seeded flesh can be added to applesauce to jazz it up. In traditional Persian cuisine, the cornelian cherry is used to flavor rice and makes a classic tart, refreshing sorbet. They call it cherry sorbet, but one taste and you know it's not your grandmother's sorbet. Unless your grandmother is Persian. In which case, lucky you.

These bright red cornelian cherries aren't quite ripe.

The dark red color of this fruit indicates ripeness.

SPRING　SUMMER　FALL　WINTER

# CRAB APPLE

*Malus* species

**What it is:** a deciduous flowering tree
**Where to find it:** gardens, yards, parks, roadsides
**Edible parts:** fruit

Crab apple flowers come in a wide range of colors.

## THE DETAILS

The crab apple is so popular as to be ubiquitous. The trees grow best in full sun but will tolerate part shade, although flowers and fruit will be more sparse. Blooms may be white, pink, or deep rose, and the fruit may be yellow, red, or orange. Technically, a crab apple is an apple with a diameter smaller than 2 inches. Many are face-twistingly sour and may have a mealy texture. Remember, they've been bred for looks, not taste. This may be why most people don't think of crab apple as an edible plant. Do yourself a favor and try a piece of fruit each time you pass a ripe crab apple tree; some are as crisp and tart as the best Granny Smith.

## HOW TO HARVEST

Crab apples are persistent fruit. Left unpicked, they'll hang on the tree until squirrels or birds have eaten every last one. Crab apples have a lot of pectin (which accounts for the *very* sour taste). If you're going to make jelly, pick them early, before a frost. Otherwise, let them stay on the tree to sweeten up a bit, but pick them before they start to shrivel. Most crab apples produce so much fruit, you'll be able to pick enough to cook with and still leave some to admire as they hang like jewels on the branches of your tree.

Generally, larger crab apples (top) are tastier and have better texture than smaller fruit.

## HOW TO EAT IT

If you're lucky to have crab apples with good texture, eat them raw or pickle them seasoned with cinnamon. These make a great side dish with pork and chicken. Even mealy fruit makes a superb jelly and a wine that's reminiscent of port. Cooking completely obliterates the mealiness, making crab apples perfect for tarts, cakes, pies, and applesauce. Taste before you bake, as you may want to add a little extra sugar.

SPRING   SUMMER   FALL   WINTER

# ELDERBERRY

*Sambucus canadensis* and *S. nigra* (a.k.a. *S. caerulea*)

**What it is:** a medium-sized deciduous shrub
**Where to find it:** gardens, roadsides, on the edges of woods
**Edible parts:** flowers, berries

Raw elderberries look better than they taste; cook them to accentuate their natural sugars.

## THE DETAILS

The elderberry is a generous shrub, producing edible crops twice a year: large, fragrant clusters of white flowers in spring and fruit in late summer. It grows best in full sun and moist, well-drained soil, but it will tolerate a location with partial shade, producing fewer flowers and fruit. Both of the above native species can be too large and sprawling for a small garden, unless they are regularly pruned. New cultivars have been bred for interesting foliage color (purple, chartreuse) and smaller stature, making them excellent garden plants. Their flowers and fruit are just as worthy as those of the straight species.

## HOW TO HARVEST

Collect the clusters of flat white flowers when they are fully open but before a rain. The pollen of elderflowers contains a natural yeast that's useful in fermenting elderflower champagne; this will be washed away in a storm. And be sure to leave some flowers on the shrub if you want to harvest berries later in the year.

Gather the fruit as soon as it ripens to a dark purple-blue. You'll have competition from the birds, so don't wait! Both flowers and fruit should be harvested by cutting the

The purple-leaved cultivar *Sambucus* 'Thundercloud' has pale pink flowers. Its blooms and berries are both edible.

stem of the cluster where it emerges from the branch.

## HOW TO EAT IT

Elderflowers are traditionally used in fritters, made by dipping the entire flower cluster in batter and frying. I prefer elderflower champagne: a light, bubbly, barely alcoholic beverage that tastes like summer. Elderflower liqueur (made from the European elder, *S. nigra*) is a popular cocktail ingredient. In Eastern Europe, Fanta sells an elderflower-lemon soda called Shokata. The most delicate and surprising way I've ever tasted elderflower? Infused in cream to make panna cotta. Amazing.

Berries are often plentiful, so it's easy to gather enough for jellies, wine, and pies. The clusters of fruit can be so heavy they bend the shrub's branches almost to the ground. Raw berries taste slightly bitter or tannic, but cooked fruit is sweet and mild and has an excellent deep purple color. Elderberry wine is a jewel-toned classic. To preserve this signature color and zip up the taste, combine with tart dark fruit such as Oregon grape (page 108) or chokeberry (page 80). Elderberry and sumac juices blend to make a delicious jelly.

Elderberries are high in antioxidants, as are other dark-fleshed small fruits such as blueberries and blackberries. Numerous studies around the world show these antioxidants to have therapeutic value when included in the human diet. Since this isn't my area of expertise, I focus on the deliciousness of the fruit and the beauty of the plant.

While some flowers are still in bloom, others have started to mature into fruit (center cluster).

SPRING   SUMMER   FALL   WINTER

# HAWTHORN

*Crataegus* species

**What it is:** a medium-sized deciduous flowering tree
**Where to find it:** gardens, parks
**Edible parts:** fruit, young leaves

Hawthorn fruit is plentiful and highly ornamental.

## THE DETAILS

The hawthorn is another tree grown primarily as an ornamental, but all species have edible fruit. Fragrant white flowers and persistent orange or red berries make it interesting throughout the growing season. And while fall foliage isn't its most outstanding characteristic, it's a very nice bright yellow. Recent cultivars are available with pink flowers. It's an adaptable tree, tolerating a range of soil quality and moisture levels. It will flower and fruit most prolifically in full sun.

## HOW TO HARVEST

Hawthorn fruit is highly variable in taste, so sample a few before you collect a bucketful. And remember, they don't call it haw*thorn* for nothing . . . Beware as you pick! Clusters of fruit are tucked in among sharp thorns, except on the few cultivars that have been bred to be thornless. Young hawthorn leaves can be used in salads, but there are more interesting salad greens out there.

## HOW TO EAT IT

Yes, you could make jelly from hawthorn berries. Or fruit leather. Or wine, or liqueur. In China, the fruit is the primary ingredient in several traditional candies. In Mexico, the berries of *Crataegus mexicana* are known as *tejocotes,* and their pulp is the base for a hot Christmas punch. Combined with chiles and other spices, it makes a candy called *rielitos dulce.*

One of my favorite hawthorn recipes is for a savory ketchup-type sauce. Combine a pound of hawthorn fruit with a cup of vinegar and simmer on low for about a half hour, then mash and sieve. Sample the pulp and add sugar to taste. (For a savory sauce, you will probably need only ¼ to ⅓ cup

Hawthorn fruits resemble small crab apples, but with different leaves and thorns.

> In China, the fruit is the primary ingredient in several traditional candies. In Mexico, the berries of *Crataegus mexicana* are known as *tejocotes,* and their pulp is the base for a hot Christmas punch.

sugar.) Add a little salt and pepper or some ground spicebush berries, and refrigerate. It's an excellent condiment for meat and fish, and certainly one you won't find in any grocery store.

Hawthorn fruit and leaves have a long history of use in herbal medicine (both Western and Eastern) as a heart tonic.

I'm not expert enough in this area to comment. I have found one reference to the seeds being dangerous because they contain cyanide. If this worries you, then use only the strained juice. But remember, apple seeds also contain cyanide; we've all swallowed a few of those and lived to tell the tale.

# HIGHBUSH CRANBERRY
## *Viburnum trilobum*

**What it is:** a medium-sized deciduous shrub
**Where to find it:** gardens, parks, woods
**Edible parts:** berries

### THE DETAILS

Viburnums are popular flowering shrubs that work well in a mixed garden. While some are prized for their round clusters of overpoweringly fragrant flowers, others like highbush cranberry produce more subdued lacecap blooms, followed by ruby-red berries. The maple-shaped leaves of this viburnum turn red in fall. The fruit is persistent and lasts well into winter, unless local birds and squirrels find your shrubbery. Highbush cranberry grows best in sun to part sun and moist, well-drained soil. Make sure you have the right plant, though. *Viburnum trilobum* is a North American native. Its European cousin, *V. opulus*, is also nicknamed highbush cranberry and looks almost exactly the same as *V. trilobum*. Sadly, its fruit tastes terrible.

### HOW TO HARVEST

The timing of your highbush cranberry harvest influences the berries'

It's tempting to leave these jewel-toned berries on the shrub so that you can admire their beauty, but they're equally wonderful in the kitchen.

characteristics. Conventional wisdom says frost makes most berries sweeter, and with crab apples or mountain ash berries you're better off letting them be nipped by a frost or two to sweeten the taste. But highbush cranberries are better picked as soon as they ripen. Then, they're sweeter, juicier, and have more pectin, making them tastier and easier to work with for jams and jellies. Freeze the berries after picking, then thaw them to make juicing easier.

If you can't get to your highbush cranberries right away, they're still worth harvesting, however. They'll hang on their branches like tiny jewels for a few months before the birds take them all away.

Now because there are bad-tasting highbush cranberries and good-tasting ones, you'll want to be sure of what you've got before you cook up a batch of anything. Even your neighborhood garden center can make a labeling mistake, and the truth

The delicate lacecap flowers of highbush cranberry add ornamental value to this native plant.

is that some botanists think the two plants may be varieties of a single species. The most reliable way to tell the difference is to just try one. But be forewarned: tasting *V. opulus* will make you want to spit. Its berries have a funky, musty taste that reminds me of sweaty workout clothes that have sat, wadded up, at the bottom of your gym bag too long. Doesn't that make you want to run out and sample one?

## HOW TO EAT IT

Highbush cranberry is not a true cranberry (*Vaccinium* species). But like the true cranberry, highbush cranberry is an intensely sour fruit. It also has a large, bitter-tasting seed. Boiling the fruit imparts some of this bitter taste from the seed, so if you're heating the fruit to make jelly (or jam, or syrup, or sauce), don't let it boil. Mash and strain the fruit (either fresh, or frozen and then thawed) and discard the seeds. Once the seed has been separated from the pulp, you can cook it as you wish. The high pectin content makes jelling easy, but why stop there? Combine the pulp and juice with sugar, orange juice, and orange zest to make a unique highbush cranberry sauce for your holiday table.

SPRING    SUMMER    FALL    WINTER

# JAPANESE QUINCE, FLOWERING QUINCE

## *Chaenomeles japonica, C. superba,* and *C. speciosa*

**What it is:** a showy, spring-flowering deciduous shrub
**Where to find it:** sunny gardens
**Edible parts:** fruit

Beware the fierce thorns that guard the ornamental quince.

## THE DETAILS

Flowering quince is grown for its highly ornamental flowers, unlike the true quince (*Cydonia oblonga*), which is grown for its large (head-of-a-baby-sized) fruit. The flowers of Japanese quince are traditionally deep coral or orange, but new cultivars come in red and pink. Be sure to read your plant tags carefully. Some new varieties have been bred to not form fruit.

These are thorny shrubs; they make an excellent hedge when planted close together. Most people assume the fruit is inedible, probably because they tried biting into one as a child. Raw, the fruit is rock hard and so sour that if you managed to take a bite you'd spit it out before it got past your teeth. Cooked is an entirely different story.

## HOW TO HARVEST

Leave fruit on the branch until it starts to fall of its own accord. This can be as late as October or November in the Northeast. Often the fruit will be marred with black spots, but these can be cut away during food preparation. The fruit is highly fragrant and will perfume your kitchen with a sweet smell somewhere between apple and pear.

## HOW TO EAT IT

Flowering quince is a great jelly fruit; it contains *lots* of natural pectin. For beginning jelly-makers who have yet to witness a crystal-clear demonstration of the jelling point, the quince is an excellent fruit. Use it for your first no-pectin-added jelly. It reaches the jelling point quickly and produces a jelly with a bright lemon

> The fruit is highly fragrant and will perfume your kitchen with a sweet smell somewhere between apple and pear.

Vibrant quince flowers stand out in the landscape.

taste. Cook it a few hours longer to make quince paste (a.k.a. membrillo, see recipe on page 210), then slice and serve with manchego cheese.

You can poach quinces in wine and spices (in a 350°F oven for 1 to 2 hours) or toss them in a slow cooker to make quince sauce. Be sure to taste as you go; you'll need more sugar than you would for applesauce. Soaked in vodka, quinces make a delicious liqueur that's high in vitamin C. I drink to your health!

Cut away black spots and remove seeds before processing quince fruit.

SPRING   SUMMER   FALL   WINTER

# JUNEBERRY, SERVICEBERRY

## *Amelanchier* species

**What it is:** a medium-sized deciduous flowering tree
**Where to find it:** woods, yards, parks
**Edible parts:** berries

### THE DETAILS

This is a tree with many common names. It's frequently called

Juneberries start off pinkish purple and ripen to a deep purple-blue.

serviceberry, and there are two popular explanations for the name. You'll hear that in colonial New England, flowers signaled that the ground was finally thawed enough to bury everyone who had died over the winter (funeral service, get it?). But since the name precedes the establishment of colonial America, it is more likely that service (or sarvis) is a variation of sorbus, a related tree.

*Amelanchier* is also called Juneberry because its berries ripen in June, shadblow because its flowers ("blow" is an old-fashioned word for flower) tell you when the shad are running, and saskatoon from the Cree name for the plant. (The Canadian city was named after the plant.) There are many

species of *Amelanchier* that produce edible fruit, but not all of it is delicious. Try some before you fill a bucket with berries.

Juneberries come in both tree and shrub (multitrunk) form and are used frequently in home landscapes, primarily for their white early-spring flowers and outstanding orange-pink fall foliage. They grow well in containers, in sun, shade, or any combination of the two. More sun usually results in more flowers and fruit. Juneberries tolerate some drought. They are true four-season trees, with tasty summer berries and smooth gray bark that stands out in winter.

### HOW TO HARVEST

Why more people don't eat Juneberries is a mystery to me. The fruit is delicious, tasting something like a combination of strawberry and blueberry with a touch of almond. Berries are slightly larger than blueberries. Perhaps people make the mistake of picking them red. While red berries are edible, they are not ripe. Juneberries ripen to a dark purple-blue; this is when they are at their best — sweet, plump, and juicy. Fruit ripens over time, so it's possible to harvest from a single tree over a period of weeks. Pick only the ripest fruit, then go back and repeat until all the berries are gone. Fruit is plentiful, and seeds germinate easily. Any fruit you miss has a good chance of producing seedlings the following year.

## HOW TO EAT IT

Saskatoons (*Amelanchier alnifolia,* the western native) are now being commercially harvested in western Canada. Studies show the berries to be higher in vitamin C, protein, fiber, and iron than blueberries. So why don't more people

White flowers precede foliage in spring.

appreciate this versatile fruit? They're delicious straight from the tree (pick berry, deposit in mouth). They can be used in any way blueberries can be: smoothies, ice cream, pancakes, muffins, jams, jellies, pies, cobblers. And don't forget fruit leather, wine, sorbet, dessert sauce, syrup. Native Americans traditionally used the

dried fruit in pemmican. It's less important *how* you eat Juneberries than *that* you eat Juneberries. This fruit deserves your attention. It's a perennial crop, readily available in quantity, from a low-maintenance and popular ornamental plant, with a first-rate taste. What are you waiting for?

SPRING   SUMMER   FALL   WINTER

# JUNIPER

## *Juniperus communis*

**What it is:** an evergreen tree or shrub
**Where to find it:** gardens, yards, fields
**Edible parts:** ripe berries

These pretty juniper berries will darken when they're ripe.

## THE DETAILS

While other species of juniper also produce edible berries (technically, fleshy cones), the fruit of *Juniperus communis* is the most popular, both in alcohol (unripe, green berries are used to flavor gin) and cooking. The taste of a ripe berry (dark blue, purple, or black) is complex and salty. An unripe berry tastes just plain awful. Both ripe and unripe berries coexist on a tree; they are highly decorative and provide excellent visual interest year-round. Common juniper may be a low-growing shrub or a tall tree; it grows best in full sun. Eastern red cedar (*J. virginiana*) also produces edible berries and is the most common juniper in the eastern United States.

> The taste of a ripe berry (dark blue, purple, or black) is complex and salty. Unripe, green berries are used to flavor gin.

The color of juniper berries intensifies with drying.

## HOW TO HARVEST

Berries take several years to ripen. They have a very strong taste and should be used in moderation. Which means you can pick plenty for the kitchen and leave ample fruit for the birds. Taste a single berry before collecting a bunch. Some trees produce juicier, tastier fruit than others.

Berries can be dried and stored for up to a year, but fresh berries have a stronger taste.

## HOW TO EAT IT

Juniper berries are a key ingredient in classic sauerkraut recipes. Just 5 to 10 berries are enough to flavor an entire batch. They are also used extensively in northern European cuisine to flavor game meats, beef, lamb, and pork. Coarsely ground with a mortar and pestle, juniper berries make a superb dry rub. Sprinkle some on a plump duck breast, and the seasoning melds with the fatty layer to form an exquisite, crisp, spicy combination.

Look beneath the evergreen foliage for tasty fruit.

SPRING    SUMMER    FALL    WINTER

# KOUSA DOGWOOD

*Cornus kousa*

**What it is:** a deciduous flowering tree
**Where to find it:** gardens, parks
**Edible parts:** fruit

This familiar flowering tree yields a tasty fruit.

## THE DETAILS

The kousa dogwood is a popular ornamental flowering tree, and rightly so. It may be single or multi-stemmed and produces showy bracts (most people think they're flowers) in white or pink. It grows best in full to part sun with reliable soil moisture, and it's resistant to the debilitating anthracnose disease that devastates our native dogwood (*Cornus florida*). Fall foliage is an appealing deep red. In late summer, the kousa dogwood produces cherry-sized fruit with dark, rosy pink, alligator-textured skin. The yellow-orange flesh of these fruits is soft and sweet. *Cornus capitata* is a less hardy *Cornus kousa* on steroids with golf-ball-sized, equally delicious fruit.

In the center of white bracts, the immature kousa fruit is visible.

## HOW TO HARVEST

The fruit is highly ornamental and is often produced in profusion. If this is the case, you'll be able to leave some on the tree for beauty's sake and harvest the rest for culinary purposes. Before you pick yourself a gallon of fruit, taste one or two. The taste and texture vary greatly from tree to tree. The best kousa fruit is juicy, sweet, and vaguely tropical (banana + melon + strawberry), while the worst is mealy and flavorless.

## HOW TO EAT IT

Kousa dogwood fruit is tasty as a snack right off the tree. Each fruit contains several medium-sized seeds, and the skin is tough. The best way to eat them is to squeeze the fruit between two fingers and squirt the flesh into your mouth, spitting out the seeds. Alternatively, pull apart the skin and suck out the flesh (again, discarding the seeds). Kousa fruit can be run through a food mill, and the flesh can be used as a side dish like applesauce. It requires very little sweetening.

Cooked, kousa fruit loses some of its taste, so while you'll read recipes for kousa jam and jelly, I prefer to eat mine raw. Some people claim cooking actually turns the fruit bitter, but I have not found that to be the case. Perhaps this can be attributed to the variability of the fruit itself.

> In late summer, the kousa dogwood produces cherry-sized fruit with dark, rosy pink, alligator-textured skin. The yellow-orange flesh of these fruits is soft and sweet.

The rosy pink fruit is ready to eat; the yellow fruit needs more time to ripen.

SPRING   SUMMER   FALL   WINTER

# MAYAPPLE

*Podophyllum peltatum*

**What it is:** an ephemeral perennial plant
**Where to find it:** gardens, woods
**Edible parts:** ripe fruit only! All other parts are poisonous.

## THE DETAILS

Many people fear the mayapple because of its reputation as a poisonous plant. In fact, the tomato plant is also poisonous; the only part that's safe to eat is the ripe fruit, just like the mayapple. Eat the right plant part at the right time and you'll be fine.

Mayapples have large leaves that are held perpendicular to their stems, forming an umbrella. The foliage, with its notched edges, is reason enough to grow this plant; it makes an interesting ground cover. Immature plants produce one leaf, and mature plants produce two, whose stems meet in a V. Below this V is where a large, bright white flower appears in early spring, hidden from view unless you get down on your knees to look. The flower gives way to a fruit, which will ripen to the size of a golf ball, with a pale yellow skin.

Mayapple spreads in dappled light along the borders of fields and woods.

Mayapples grow best in part shade and moist soil. Their foliage turns yellow in summer, dying back at about the same time the fruit ripens. Plants remain dormant until early spring the following year.

## HOW TO HARVEST

Check your mayapple plants regularly! Humans aren't the only hungry animals who know the ripe fruit is delicious. Deer, raccoons, and squirrels leave the foliage alone but will steal the fruit out from under you. Some references say mayapples will ripen on a kitchen windowsill if they're harvested when the first tint of yellow starts to show. I find fruit picked this young never develops its full rich flavor or soft texture, so I encourage you to leave it on the plant as long as possible — until it's fully yellow and soft to the touch. Then cut the fruit's stem and leave the plant in place.

## HOW TO EAT IT

I won't lie to you: it's unusual to find enough mayapples to make something substantial.

Fruit may abort during the growing season if conditions aren't absolutely perfect, leaving a large grove of mayapples with just a handful of fruit. Fortunately, it's so delicious you'll be grateful for even a single one. Cut the fruit in half and scoop the flesh out of the bitter skins. The seeds are large-ish; you'll probably want to spit them out. But if you swallow a stray seed you're perfectly safe.

If you're lucky enough to harvest a bonanza, run the scooped flesh through a food mill and use it for jam, sorbet, or pie. Juice can be drunk plain or used for jelly. The color and taste are the embodiment of tropical sunshine: pale yellow and indescribably complex and sweet.

Mayapple flowers give way to fruit . . . if you're lucky! Note that the fruit ripens just as the foliage fades.

SPRING SUMMER FALL WINTER

# MAYPOP, PASSIONFLOWER

## *Passiflora incarnata* and *P. caerulea*

**What it is:** a perennial vine
**Where to find it:** gardens, roadsides
**Edible parts:** ripe fruit

## THE DETAILS

A close relative of the tropical passionfruit vine, this passionflower is hardy to Zone 7. (Some people claim it's hardy to Zone 6, but my experience says not really.) In the South, growth can be so rampant that the plant is sometimes thought of as a weed, but elsewhere it's a plant much appreciated for its large, intricate purple-and-white flowers. The vine grows best in full sun and well-drained soils and is drought tolerant once established. It grows well in containers and can easily cover 15 to 25 feet in a few months. If your growing season is long enough, fruit matures to the size of an egg. It may be green or yellow with pale yellow pulp surrounding numerous seeds inside. In warmer climates, blue passionflower (*P. caerulea*) ripens to a bright orange color with red pulp inside.

After flowering, this *Passiflora incarnata* will produce fruit that ripens to a greenish yellow, with pale yellow flesh inside.

## HOW TO HARVEST

Ripe fruit will be soft when it's ready to pick. It will subsequently fall from the vine, so keep your eye on the fruit and your window of opportunity. The ripe fruit is soft and juicy and will either smoosh or crack open when it falls, thus becoming useless to you.

## HOW TO EAT IT

The seed-to-pulp ratio of maypop is unfortunately high, so making maypop juice is an excellent way to take advantage of its natural sweetness. Blue passionflower produces a more strikingly beautiful ruby-toned juice, but both species taste great.

Cut the fruit in half (or pull it open with your fingers . . . it's that soft) and scoop the seeds and pulp into a shallow pan, discarding the skin. Add barely enough water to cover, then simmer, mash, and strain, as described for prickly pear on page 115.

If you want to taste the raw fruit, pop a seed into your mouth. Each one is surrounded by a small covering of fruit, much like pomegranate seeds. Kind of a lot of work, if you ask me.

The fruit of this passionflower (*P. caerulea*) is ripe and ready to pick.

The ruby red flesh of passionfruit yields a sweet juice.

SPRING SUMMER FALL WINTER

# MOUNTAIN ASH, ROWAN

## *Sorbus americana* and *S. alnifolia*

**What it is:** a small, ornamental deciduous tree
**Where to find it:** yards, parks, woods
**Edible parts:** berries

Orange fruit and feathery foliage make for an attractive tree.

## THE DETAILS

The mountain ash tree grows best in cool climates, full sun, and moist soil. It will not tolerate drought or warmer habitats, although it grows south of Zone 6 at altitudes that provide cool temperatures. In all cases, the mountain ash is a relatively short-lived tree, rarely passing 30 years in age. It's popular in the landscape, appreciated for its finely cut leaves and bright yellow fall foliage. Large clusters of fragrant white flowers appear in late spring to early summer, but the fruit is its most ornamental aspect. Abundant berries are produced in fall and persist through the winter months, providing food for birds and small mammals. Fruit is usually bright orange or red, although cultivars exist with white,

*Sorbus alnifolia* has foliage that resembles that of the alder.

yellow, and pink berries. Most humans mistakenly think these are poisonous. Related species produce similar fruit.

## HOW TO HARVEST

Since the berries are the most ornamental aspect of this tree, it's tempting to leave them on the branches for a visual feast. Fruit becomes sweeter after a frost, so don't pick until temperatures drop below freezing, then harvest as many berries as you need. If you must pick before a frost, freeze the berries before using them to mellow their astringent taste. And don't forget to leave some behind for the birds.

## HOW TO EAT IT

Raw berries are juicy and highly astringent; they also contain parasorbic acid, which can cause indigestion. Cooking converts parasorbic acid to sorbic acid, which is entirely benign. The cooked fruit makes a tasty, not overly sweet jelly with a bright orange color, traditionally used as an accompaniment to meat. The berries have plenty of pectin, so you can ignore the recipes that recommend adding packaged pectin. It simply isn't necessary, and the jelly has a better taste and texture without it. Mountain ash berries can also be used to make wine and to flavor liqueurs. A combination of freezing the berries before using, and cooking them in preparation for use, will give you the tastiest results. Food and beverages made from mountain ash juice are beautiful to look at and have a unique sweet-tart taste.

> Fruit becomes sweeter after a frost, so don't pick until temperatures drop below freezing, then harvest as many berries as you need.

The bright color of mountain ash berries makes a jewel-toned jelly.

SPRING　SUMMER　FALL　WINTER

# MULBERRY

## *Morus* species

**What it is:** a large deciduous tree
**Where to find it:** yards, parks, roadsides
**Edible parts:** berries, leaves

The easiest way to tell when mulberries are ripe is to look at the ground below the tree, *not* at the fruit!

## THE DETAILS

Red, white, and black mulberries are three individual species of tree, each producing edible fruit. These trees are often considered weeds, and seedlings do sprout readily from the many berries that fall to the ground and remain there, uneaten and unappreciated. Mulberries are unusual in that they produce three different leaf shapes on a single tree, much like the sassafras tree. They grow in sun to part shade. Mulberries have been cultivated for thousands of years. In the myth of Pyramus and Thisbe (an ancient story of tragic love, similar to that of Romeo and Juliet) the blood of Pyramus turns the white mulberry red. That's a lot of drama for a fruit.

> Red and black mulberries have a stronger taste than white mulberries, but all three are delicious raw over ice cream, with a drizzle of excellent balsamic vinegar.

The dark purple berry is ripe, the red needs a few days, and the white fruit will be ripe in about a week.

## HOW TO HARVEST

Mulberries will tell you when they're ripe. If you're walking down the street (or across your patio) and you notice numerous messy splotches on the pavement, look up. There may be ripe mulberries just overhead. Ripe fruit is *very* soft, which is probably why they aren't found in most grocery stores; shipping would be problematic. The slightest touch makes a ripe berry fall into your hand. If you have to pull, even a little, it isn't ready. In your backyard, spread a tarp under the mulberry tree and shake the trunk, then collect your bounty. Fruit ripens over a period of a few weeks, so you'll want to harvest several times. And for your information, red mulberries are actually dark purple when ripe. Go figure.

I've read that young mulberry leaves are edible both raw in salads and cooked as a vegetable. I have never bothered to try this because no one has said they are delicious. Life is too short to waste on mere sustenance.

## HOW TO EAT IT

I am baffled that so many people describe the mulberry's taste as insipid. I find the fruit sweet and juicy, and every year I wish I had more. There's an ancient recipe for a honey wine made with mulberries (it's called morat) that I'd love to try, but I've never had enough fruit.

Red and black mulberries have a stronger taste than white mulberries, but all three are delicious raw over ice cream, with a drizzle of excellent balsamic vinegar. They combine well with more acidic fruit in pies, jams, and jellies. Try them with rhubarb, gooseberries, currants, cornelian cherries, or Oregon grapes.

SPRING  SUMMER  FALL  WINTER

# OREGON GRAPE

## *Mahonia aquifolium,* a.k.a. *Berberis aquifolium*

**What it is:** a small to medium-sized broadleaf evergreen shrub
**Where to find it:** gardens, woods
**Edible parts:** ripe berries

### THE DETAILS

This popular landscape shrub grows best in shade to part shade. The leaves resemble holly leaves in their sharpness, and new foliage emerges with a red tint. Upright sprays of yellow flowers give way to purple-blue fruit, and like their namesake these "grapes" are covered with a whitish bloom, which is a natural yeast. The fruit is intensely sour. *Mahonia repens* is a ground cover that also produces edible fruit. Both species are quite drought tolerant once established, but they will flower and

Oregon grape's evergreen leaves are attractive all year long. Its flowers open up to a bright yellow.

> Oregon grapes have more pectin before a frost but are sweeter after a frost, so how you plan to use the fruit will determine when you pick them.

fruit more reliably with regular water. Oregon grape foliage is vulnerable to winter desiccation and should be planted away from drying winter winds.

## HOW TO HARVEST

Oregon grapes have more pectin before a frost but are sweeter after a frost, so how you plan to use the fruit will determine when you pick them. The flowers are more intensely decorative, since their bright yellow color is visible from a greater distance, than the more subtly colored fruit. I suggest enjoying the beauty of the flowers, then harvesting the fruit after it has ripened, but before your first frost.

Like true grapes, the fruit of Oregon grape is covered with a white bloom that contains natural yeast.

## HOW TO EAT IT

The ripe berries are edible raw, but most are so sour you probably won't enjoy them this way. Still, if you're feeling brave, taste one straight off the shrub and see what you think. You'll probably want to spit out the sizable seeds. Pre-frost Oregon grapes make an excellent jelly, requiring no additional pectin. Their intense tartness persists despite the addition of sugar, making the taste especially interesting. Oregon grapes harvested after a frost can be used for wine (if you have a lot of fruit), ice cream, pies, or fruit leather. I like to combine them with sweeter, mellower fruit to create a hedgerow fruit leather. This can be eaten as is, or rehydrated to make a base for fruit sauce, sweet or savory.

SPRING  SUMMER  FALL  WINTER

# PINEAPPLE GUAVA

*Acca sellowiana,* a.k.a. *Feijoa sellowiana*

**What it is:** a multistemmed, medium-sized deciduous shrub
**Where to find it:** regions where winter temperatures stay above 10°F; sun to part shade; drought tolerant
**Edible parts:** petals, fruit

Pineapple guava pulp is extremely versatile. It can be used in pies, breads, ice cream, jam, smoothies, or salsa. Use the juice for jelly or syrup, or make a light and refreshing agua fresca.

## THE DETAILS

This is a popular ornamental shrub with showy edible flowers. It responds well to pruning and can be shaped easily. It's often used as a hedge and makes a good espalier. Gray-green leaves are silvery underneath, and the flowers are large and unusual. Petals are white on the outside, pink or white inside, and at the center of the flower are masses of bright red stamens tipped with creamy yellow anthers. Fruit is blue-green, egg-shaped, and 1 to 3 inches long. All that, and it has orangey, exfoliating bark,

Pineapple guava makes an impressive living fence.

too! It's drought tolerant and grows best in a fast-draining soil. Pineapple guavas are grudgingly self-fertile, but planting two or more will result in better pollination and a larger crop.

## HOW TO HARVEST

The fleshy petals can be pulled *carefully* off the flower and eaten. The center of the flower (including the ovary, which will become the fruit) must be left intact. Pineapple guava petals have more substance than most flowers and are sweet and spicy. They can be used as garnish, in salads, or as a snack out of hand.

Fruit falls from the tree when it's ripe. In the United States, this is in fall, or as late as December in Northern California. It's strongly fragrant, even before it's ready to pick. Since the fruit is similar in color to the foliage, you may smell it before you see it. Size is not an indicator of ripeness. Ripe fruit can be as large as a small lemon or smaller than a golf ball. Don't be tempted

If you pluck the edible petals carefully, you won't disturb the ripening fruit.

to pick fruit from the tree! If harvested too early, the full flavor of the fruit won't develop. So wait until the fruit actually falls to the ground, then collect it. Ripe fruit lasts well in the refrigerator for up to a month. It's possible to collect vast quantities of this fruit; the shrubs are large and prolific, and most people leave the fruit to rot. What a shame.

## HOW TO EAT IT

Try this fruit fresh from the tree, so you can get a handle on its unique, tropical taste. The flesh is greenish white. The many small seeds are edible, although the peel is not; cut the fruit in half and scoop out the flesh. If you're not going to use the cut or peeled fruit right away, treat as you would cut or peeled apples, submerging in water with lemon juice or citric acid to prevent the exposed flesh from turning brown.

Pineapple guava pulp is extremely versatile. It can be used in pies, breads, ice cream, jam, smoothies, or salsa. Use the juice for jelly or syrup, or make a light and refreshing *agua fresca* (see recipe on page 222). The pulp stores well frozen.

# PRICKLY PEAR

## *Opuntia* species

**What it is:** a cactus
**Where to find it:** gardens, roadsides, *not* just in the desert!
**Edible parts:** fruit, pads

A prickly pear, entwined by a neighboring vine, bears ripening fruits.

## THE DETAILS

Yes, the prickly pear is a classic desert plant, but many species of this plant grow across the continental United States and into Canada. Not surprisingly, they grow best in full sun and sandy, fast-draining soil. Large, showy flowers may be yellow, white, or pink. In locations with cold winters, cactus pads fall to the ground and turn mushy. Let them sit; these may sprout in spring, resulting in more prickly pears for you.

## HOW TO HARVEST

Do I need to say "carefully!"? *Opuntia* species have varying degrees of armor. Cactus pads are covered with *areoles* — tan-colored bumps from which grow both obvious spines and almost invisible, usually barbed *glochids*. Glochids detach from the plant easily, with the mere brush of a hand. They are hard to see and even harder to remove. Glochids are easy to feel, however, and it isn't a good feeling. Prickly pear fruit is similarly well protected.

Gloves are essential for harvesting prickly pear!

Whether you're harvesting pads or fruit, wear leather gloves and use tongs. Fruit can be twisted off the plant. Cut pads with a sharp knife, leaving about an inch of the bottom of the pad behind. New growth will emerge from there. Spines and glochids can be scraped off with a knife or a vegetable peeler, or singed off by holding the pads or fruit over a flame. If you use the fire method, you'll still want to peel the tough skin from the pad or fruit before cooking with it.

## HOW TO EAT IT

Prickly pear pads are called *nopales* in Mexican cuisine, and they are delicious in a green-bean, bell-pepper kind of way. After removing the spines, glochids, and skin, slice the pads, chop, and cook with onions or garlic, then use them in egg dishes, stews, soups, or as a vegetable side dish. This is a highly mucilaginous

Shockingly magenta *tunas* yield a gorgeous juice.

vegetable (puts okra to shame); better to eat it cooked than raw.

Prickly pear fruit are called *tunas*. When ripe they may be red, purple, orange, or yellow, and barely soft to the touch. Depending on your cooking plans, you may want to peel and seed the tunas. Cut off the top and bottom of the fruit, then make a slit along its length. You should be able to lift and peel off the skin (again, with tongs) in a single piece.

If you're going to use the juice only (and not the pulp), there's no need to skin the fruit. Just cut it in quarters, barely cover with water, then simmer

Prickly pear pads (a.k.a. *nopales*) should be peeled before cooking.

for about 10 minutes and mash to release the juices. Strain the juice, then proceed with jelly, syrup, or sorbet.

Cooked tuna flesh turns a shade of magenta that is so intense it seems artificial. It makes a gorgeous jelly, jam, syrup, sorbet, or *agua fresca* (see recipe on page 222); if you've got a large crop, you could even try making a gallon of cactus wine. The taste is unusual and difficult to describe in terms of other fruit. Kind of like a watermelon-apple hybrid, but with extra texture. Better you should try for yourself.

> After removing the spines, glochids, and skin, slice the pads, chop, and cook with onions or garlic. Prickly pear fruit tastes kind of like a watermelon-apple hybrid, but with extra texture.

SPRING    SUMMER    FALL    WINTER

# REDBUD
## *Cercis canadensis*

**What it is:** a small to medium-sized deciduous flowering tree
**Where to find it:** woods, yards, parks
**Edible parts:** flower buds

## THE DETAILS

The redbud is a much-loved ornamental tree. Before leaves emerge in spring, its branches are literally covered with bright pink buds, which just happen to be edible! Its foliage is heart-shaped, and new leaves have a reddish tint. Later on, trees provide showy, yellow fall foliage. New cultivars have been bred with fantastic foliage. 'Forest Pansy' and 'Merlot' produce purple leaves, and the foliage of 'Hearts of Gold' is char-treuse. Redbuds have a low-branching vase shape, but several weeping cultivars offer unusual architectural interest. Redbuds grow best in part shade, although they'll tolerate full sun in loca-tions with cooler summers. Though they require good soil moisture, they grow in a range of soils from clay to sand and also do well in containers. These are excellent trees with one shortcoming: they are generally short-lived, rarely lasting more than 30 years in the landscape.

## HOW TO HARVEST

Collect buds when they're tightly closed. Of course you'll want to leave some buds in place so you can enjoy their bloom, but the redbud is so floriferous you can have your flowers and eat them, too. Even if you picked every other bud, you'd still have plenty to look at on the tree.

I've read several accounts of people using the young green seed-pods like snow peas (the redbud is a member of the pea family), but I can't recommend this from personal experience. I've tried them raw and boiled and found them tough, stringy, and ultimately

**EASY I.D.**
Nothing else looks like a redbud. Magenta flowers emerge from the trunk and branches before foliage unfurls, blan-keting the wood in bloom.

> **Before leaves emerge in spring, its branches are literally covered with bright pink buds, which just happen to be edible!**

Redbud flowers make this tree a standout in early spring.

unsatisfying. Perhaps a different climate produces a more tender pod. They're edible, certainly, but are they worth it? Depends on what else you have to eat. The pods definitely don't live up to my standards of deliciousness.

## HOW TO EAT IT

Raw redbud buds add a snappy crunch to salads, either sprinkled on top of leafy greens or mixed into potato salad (or chicken salad, or tuna salad). They have a fresh, tart taste that combines well with both sweet and savory dishes. Sprinkle them on ice cream or yogurt; their bright pink color offers visual punch as well as a satisfying chew. Cooked buds can be added to muffins, breads, and vegetable stir-fries, although their color fades with the application of heat. If you're really ambitious or have way too much spare time, dip the opened flowers in tempura batter and deep-fry them. Then call me, because you are my kind of person and I'm coming over for lunch.

# ROSE OF SHARON

## *Hibiscus syriacus*

**What it is:** a small to medium-sized deciduous shrub, very floriferous
**Where to find it:** gardens, parks
**Edible parts:** leaves, flowers

Familiar shrub or surprising edible?

## THE DETAILS

Rose of Sharon is a traditional and much-loved flowering shrub. It grows best in full sun but will tolerate part shade, although with less light it produces fewer blooms. Flowers may be single or double and come in white, pink, or purple-blue. Rose of Sharon leafs out late in the season and blooms at the end of summer. Once established, it can tolerate some drought. Young leaves are edible raw, as are its flower petals.

## HOW TO HARVEST

If you need a few leaves for your salad, prune or pinch off the youngest leaves just above a node. The foliage doesn't have a special taste, but it's safe to eat and will fill up your salad bowl. Rose of Sharon's flowers are much

The large flowers make excellent vessels for soft cheese mixtures.

more visually and texturally interesting than its foliage. Picked early in the day, before they're fully open, the flowers will be crisp, fresh, and mild. Because Rose of Sharon produces so many flowers, you don't have to worry about picking your shrub bare. There'll be plenty to look at *and* to nibble.

## HOW TO EAT IT

Individual petals can be used whole or chopped in salads, cold soups, or gelatin molds. Since Rose of Sharon flowers are larger than many other edible flowers, they can be stuffed and served as hors d'oeuvres. Remove the pistils and stamens, leaving the petals in an open cup. In a blender, combine yogurt and cream or cottage cheese, then make it sweet (with honey, dried fruit, slivered almonds) or savory (with scallions, thyme, pine nuts), and drop a dollop into the center of each petal cup. Arranged on a platter, these stuffed flowers are an unusual, elegant offering for afternoon tea.

SPRING  SUMMER  FALL  WINTER

# RUGOSA ROSE

*Rosa rugosa*

**What it is:** an old-fashioned deciduous flowering shrub
**Where to find it:** gardens, beaches
**Edible parts:** hips and petals

> Pick rose hips after they've turned red and before they start to wrinkle. If you can wait until after a frost, they'll be sweeter. Hips can be frozen until you have time to work with them.

## THE DETAILS

The truth is that any rose that hasn't been sprayed with hideous chemicals yields edible flowers. Without fragrance, though, there's not much reason to eat a rose petal. The petal itself doesn't have much taste, but a scented petal brings something interesting to the table. Sadly, many of today's hybrid roses have had all the scent bred out of them, focusing instead on flower color and size. I spurn them all. Any rose worthy of the name must have a seductive scent. And big hips don't hurt. This is why the rugosa rose is so welcome in the kitchen. Its blooms (in white, pink, or magenta) are strongly scented, and it produces the largest hips of any rose I know.

Bright red rose hips are especially ornamental in winter.

In fall, its foliage turns bright yellow. Rugosa rose is especially prickly, but deliciousness is worth a little suffering.

All roses grow best in full sun and well-drained soil. Good air circulation helps keep foliar diseases at bay. Rugosa rose is especially disease resistant and also salt tolerant, making it a useful planting along roads and beaches.

## HOW TO HARVEST

Harvesting both flowers and fruit from the same rose is tricky, but it can be done. While it's possible to remove only the petals from a flower, leaving the center of the rose behind to form fruit, remember that it's the petals that attract pollinators. Without petals, the flower may not be appealing enough to lure the essential bee. You're better off harvesting every second or third flower for petals, leaving the rest behind to form fruit.

Pick flowers just after they've opened, while petals are still firm and fresh. Trim off the white ends of each petal (where they joined the base of the flower); these can be bitter.

Pick rose hips after they've turned red and before they start to wrinkle. If you can wait until after a frost, they'll be sweeter. Hips can be frozen until you have time to work with them.

## HOW TO EAT IT

Rose hips contain many tiny seeds, which are surrounded by itchy hairs that can stick in your throat. (These hairs were used to make the original itching powder. Cool, huh?) So please, don't just bite into a raw rose hip. To eat the raw fruit, first cut it in half, scrape out the seeds, and discard them. The outer fruit is now safe to eat. If you plan to make rose hip jelly or syrup, there's no need to remove the seeds. Go ahead and process the fruit as you would any other, simmering in minimal water and straining through cheesecloth or a jelly bag. If you want pulp rather than juice, remove the seeds (see above) before processing the fruit

Rugosa roses come in shades of pink and white and have the biggest hips of any rose.

for jam, sauce, fruit leather, soup, or pudding.

Rose petals are often used as garnish or in salads, but I think their sweet, spicy fragrance cries out to be dessert. How about rose petal ice cream with rose petal syrup? Purée petals in a food processor to get pulp. For ice cream, substitute the petal pulp for fruit pulp in your favorite ice cream recipe. For syrup, add 1 part pulp to 2 parts simple syrup and simmer until it reaches the desired thickness. Strain before using.

SPRING  SUMMER  FALL  WINTER

# SILVERBERRY, AUTUMN OLIVE

## *Elaeagnus umbellata*

**What it is:** a large deciduous shrub, often a volunteer
**Where to find it:** roadsides, fields, yards
**Edible parts:** berries

## THE DETAILS

Hundreds of these shrubs were planted as windbreaks and for erosion control before landscape designers realized how invasive they could be. The extraordinarily large amount of fruit produced by each shrub, combined with an enviably successful germination rate, means that once you have one silverberry, you're likely to have more.

Silverberry fruit is plentiful and versatile.

It tolerates poor, dry soils and requires almost no care, although it produces more fruit in sunnier locations. The undersides of its leaves are silvery white, and the berries are speckled with silver. The fruit itself may be pink or red and is quite ornamental. Goumi (*Elaeagnus multiflora*) also produces worthy fruit.

## HOW TO HARVEST

Silverberry fruit is soft when fully ripe, and premature picking yields an astringent crop, so be patient! Because the small berries are so abundant, it's possible to collect a substantial amount in a short time. I use both hands to gently roll berries off their stems, gathering the fruit until they start to spill from my fists.

Silverberries may be round or almost oblong; either way, they're flecked with silvery spots.

## HOW TO EAT IT

This is one of my favorite foraged fruits, and that's not because it's high in vitamin C and lycopene. It's tart and tasty raw (spit out the good-sized seed). When the fresh berries are run through a food mill, they make a thick, gorgeous pulp that can be swirled into yogurt or used as the base for a fruit soup. Silverberry makes a superb jelly, and wine made from silverberries is light, clean, and fruity without being too sweet. Silverberry cake is moist and delicious, and has a fantastic bright pink color.

SPRING  SUMMER  FALL  WINTER

# SPICEBUSH, APPALACHIAN ALLSPICE

*Lindera benzoin*

**What it is:** a small deciduous flowering shrub
**Where to find it:** gardens, woods
**Edible parts:** berries, leaves

Small yellow flowers yield tasty red fruit.

## THE DETAILS

This small flowering shrub is dioecious, which means there are separate male and female plants. While both produce attractive, dainty yellow flowers in early spring and bright yellow fall foliage, only the females have edible berries. So, if you'd like to plant this shrub for its fruit, do it in the fall, when berries should be evident. You'll need a male shrub for pollination, but one male can pollinate several females. Spicebush grows best in part shade.

## HOW TO HARVEST

Spicebush tea can be made from fresh or dried leaves. It has a mild, chai-like flavor that is pleasant hot or iced. Although "mild" and "pleasant" aren't two adjectives I strive for in the kitchen, many people

> Spicebush berries have a complex taste that combines well with both sweet and savory dishes. My description of "reminiscent of pepper and allspice" is pathetically inadequate.

enjoy this tea. Personally, I prefer stronger flavors.

Spicebush berries, on the other hand, are over-the-top fantastic. They should be picked as soon as they turn red. Since the fruit is relatively small (and therefore not hugely ornamental), it shouldn't break your heart to pick them off the shrub. This is such a fantastic edible that I suggest you gather as much as you can. Berries can be stored in the refrigerator for up to a week. Frozen or dehydrated, they'll keep for a year or more. Store berries whole until you're ready to use them, then grind as much as you need.

## HOW TO EAT IT

As is sometimes the case with common names, the term "spicebush" is applied to several different small shrubs. If you're planting a spicebush, please check the botanical name to be sure what you have is *Lindera benzoin*. Spicebush berries have a complex taste that combines well with both sweet and savory dishes. My description of "reminiscent of pepper and allspice" is pathetically inadequate. Please try it for yourself.

Spicebush ice cream is an excellent foil for gingersnap cookies or pumpkin pie. Spicebush is also lovely in rice pudding. It blends well with apples and pears in pies and cobblers; substitute it for cinnamon and nutmeg. A rub (dry or wet) made of equal parts spicebush berries, wild ginger, and sweetfern is magnificent on pork. Add a little salt and some brown sugar, and you'll be in heaven.

Grind the seeds and fruit together to create a complex spice.

# STRAWBERRY TREE

## *Arbutus unedo*

**What it is:** a small, drought-tolerant evergreen tree or shrub
**Where to find it:** Zones 7 to 10, in climates with dry summers
**Edible parts:** fruit

### THE DETAILS

The strawberry tree is unusual in that it simultaneously displays fruit at various stages of ripeness. White flowers, immature yellow-orange fruit, and ripe red fruit coexist on the tree in an attractive display. Fruit takes a full year to ripen. Gray, exfoliating bark reveals a cinnamon-colored underlayer; it's an attractive combination. Birds appreciate the fruit raw, but the mealy texture of the skin is a little off-putting

Flowers coexist with ripening and ripe fruit.

In the Mediterranean, cooked fruit from the strawberry tree is used in preserves and forms the base for the Portuguese brandy medronho.

to the rest of us. In the Mediterranean, however, the cooked fruit is used in preserves and forms the base for the Portuguese brandy medronho. Greek tsipouro (another alcoholic drink, stronger than ouzo) is made from grapes or strawberry tree fruit. The high pectin content of the fruit makes it a natural for jams and jellies. It is closely related to *Arbutus menziesii* (madrone, native to California), whose berries can be used in the same way.

## HOW TO HARVEST

When berries are ripe, they fall easily from the tree. If a gentle tug doesn't release the fruit, it's not ready.

You can spread a blanket or tarp under your tree and shake, to speed the harvest. Since the berries don't all ripen at once, you may need to amass your harvest in the freezer until you have enough to cook with. Wash and refrigerate the berries right away, even if you're going to use them the same day. They're very soft when fully ripe and don't keep long.

## HOW TO EAT IT

The ripe, raw flesh of strawberry tree fruit is brilliant orange. Run the raw fruit through a food mill to create a gorgeous pulp that combines the red skins with the orange

flesh. The fruit is sweet but bland; adding something acidic makes the taste much more interesting. Strawberry tree berries ripen at the same time as pomegranates and Meyer lemons; both combine well with arbutus fruit. The seeds are small and can be left in, but if the texture bothers you, press the pulp through a fine strainer. This fruit makes an excellent jam and a tasty fruit leather; the color darkens with cooking. If you're particularly flush with fruit, try making a gallon of wine.

# SUMAC

## *Rhus typhina* and *R. glabra*

**What it is:** a large deciduous shrub
**Where to find it:** gardens, yards, roadsides
**Edible parts:** berries

These bright red berries are ready to harvest.

### THE DETAILS

The common roadside sumac is one of the easiest-to-identify edible plants. In mid to late summer its deep red cones of berries make it unmistakable in the landscape, and you'll see it almost everywhere you look: roadside ditches, overgrown fields, abandoned city lots, and along the edges of woodlands. It's often found in the company of milkweed, evening primrose, and burdock, which are also edible wild plants.

Sumac can be too aggressive for some gardens, but new cultivars bred for their foliage are more demure and work well in a mixed border. They produce cones of red berries that can be used exactly like the berries of the more common roadside plants. Sumacs grow best in full sun and well-drained soils. They are often one of the first plants to take root in recently cleared spots or disturbed soils.

### HOW TO HARVEST

Timing is everything. Sumac berries get their lemony taste from a combination of acids that coat them. This is washed away by rain, so gather your sumac as soon as possible after the berries ripen. The acid re-accumulates a few days after each rain, but the berries become progressively less tart (and less tasty) with each successive downpour. Dry whole cones by placing them in a paper bag and hanging them somewhere dark and dry for 2 to 4 weeks. After that, store them whole in a large glass jar and use as needed.

Dried sumac berries are dark red.

## HOW TO EAT IT

Sumac-ade is a favorite among children; it's easy to make by breaking apart several cones of berries and adding a pitcher of water, then letting them soak until the liquid turns pink. Taste periodically to test for sourness. Cold brewing takes longer than hot brewing (hours versus minutes) but produces a tastier beverage. Strain the liquid through a jelly bag, coffee filter, or very fine mesh. The taste-producing hairs are unpleasant and scratchy in the throat, so you'll be happier if you can

Look familiar? Sumac is a very common roadside plant.

avoid them. You'll probably want to sweeten it with a little honey.

Sumac berries can be simmered and juiced, then used to make jelly. They can also be soaked in rum or vodka with a little sugar to create a tart cocktail. As with sumac-ade, you'll need to strain out the hairs before consuming.

### "SOUND-ALIKE" TO AVOID

All sumac bushes with red berries are safe to touch and eat. Poison sumac (*Toxicodendron vernix*) has creamy yellow flowers, followed by white berries. If you stay away from white-berried sumac, you'll be fine.

# Snackworthy Fruits and Flowers

There are some plants that don't exactly make a meal, but the fact that you can eat them is too interesting to be ignored. The following are a few flowers and berries that are worth snacking on in the garden, even if you wouldn't serve them as a main course.

## American beautyberry

*Callicarpa americana*

**What it is:** a medium-sized deciduous shrub

**Where to find it:** gardens, parks

**Edible parts:** berries

The purple berries are small and vaguely sweet; their texture may be juicy or mealy, depending on the luck of the draw. White-berried cultivars are also edible. Japanese beautyberry (*Callicarpa japonica*) is not recommended as an edible plant, although I've nibbled on the fruit and lived long enough to write about it. American beautyberry grows best in full to part sun and well-drained soil. Fruit is at its peak in mid to late autumn and will persist long after the leaves have fallen. Sadly, the fruit loses its color with cooking, so even though you can make beautyberry jelly, it won't keep that lovely lilac hue.

# Firethorn

*Pyracantha coccinea*

**What it is:** a well-armored evergreen or semi-evergreen shrub

**Where to find it:** gardens, parks

**Edible parts:** berries

This drought-tolerant shrub is often trained as an espalier against walls. Its fruit may be yellow, vermilion, or cherry red and is well protected by sturdy thorns. Birds love the berries, although they are a little mealy for human taste. Most people consider them too tart to eat raw, but, as often happens, a frost will sweeten the fruit. Firethorn is a traditional jelly fruit; the color of its skin dictates the color of the jelly. Firethorn jelly won't bowl you over with its unusual flavor. It tastes like a mild, sweet apple preserve. Combined with strong, tart fruits like mountain ash berries or crab apples, firethorn tones down their sour taste. Firethorn is a plentiful, underused fruit and if you have it in your garden, why not make the most of it?

# Lilac

*Syringa vulgaris*

**What it is:** a fragrant deciduous shrub

**Where to find it:** gardens, parks

**Edible parts:** flowers

With their intoxicatingly fragrant flowers, lilacs are a much-loved garden shrub. Admittedly, it's a heavy scent. I wouldn't wear it, but I sure love to stick my nose in a bunch of lilac flowers. I don't get too excited about edible blooms because generally they don't have much flavor. They're novelty items that offer visual and textural interest at best. But lilacs also bring scent to the table. My favorite way to use them is for making wine. Uncorking a bottle of lilac wine in January releases the sweet fragrance of spring. Intoxicating, indeed.

## Magnolia

*Magnolia* species

**What it is:** a deciduous (or sometimes evergreen) flowering tree

**Where to find it:** gardens, yards, parks

**Edible parts:** flowers, buds

I know, I know, I said I didn't like edible flowers, but trust me, this is no insipid bloom. Magnolia petals have a strong taste, reminiscent of clove. Not everybody likes the taste, but then again, not everybody likes tomatoes, either. Personally, I think magnolia flowers are fantastic. Tear a few fresh petals into pieces and add them to salads or use as a garnish. Or pick an unopened bud (not a fruit!) and grate it with a microplane to use as a spice. You won't need much . . . these flowers pack a spicy punch.

## Yew

*Taxus baccata*

**What it is:** an evergreen shrub

**Where to find it:** gardens, parks

**Edible parts:** the flesh of the berries ONLY!

You've probably been told that yews are deadly poisonous and it's true . . . EXCEPT for the flesh of the ripe berry. The fruit of the yew is an aril and consists of flesh surrounding a prominent seed. The ripe red flesh of the yew aril is delicious: juicy, mild, and sweet. You may never collect enough to make a sauce, jelly, or jam, but you could. I recommend them as a handy snack. Just be sure you spit out the seed!

# CHAPTER 5

# NATURE'S GRANOLA:
# Nuts and Seeds

Smooth, sweet chestnuts come in a fierce, spiky package.

# It's not a stretch to see plants as fruits and vegetables,

but most of us don't look in the backyard for proteins or fats. Yet they're there, in the form of nuts and seeds. These are some of the most nutritious and delicious plant parts there are, worth the extra work of handling a spiky chestnut husk or squeezing the seed out of a stinky ginkgo fruit.

Nuts can be eaten whole, chopped, or ground. You can roast chestnuts and eat them plain and simple, grind acorns into flour, or dig the meat out of black walnuts (after removing the husks, curing the nuts, and cracking the shells). However you eat them, nuts offer a lot of flavor in a small package.

SPRING    SUMMER    FALL    WINTER

# BLACK WALNUT

*Juglans nigra*

**What it is:** a large deciduous tree
**Where to find it:** yards, parks, woods
**Edible parts:** nuts

## THE DETAILS

Historically, black walnuts were popular shade trees, so it's not unusual to find majestic, mature specimens in yards and parks across the country. This is a classic shade tree, growing to 100 feet tall and casting a wide shadow. Because its wood is extremely highly valued for fine carpentry work, many large trees have been sacrificed. Black walnut grows best in full sun and deep, moist, well-drained soil. Its roots have an allelopathic effect on some plants, especially those in the tomato family, yet other plants grow perfectly well in the presence of black walnut.

## HOW TO HARVEST

Now it gets interesting. Black walnuts can be harvested while still on the tree, but it's easier to wait until they start to fall. Collect the green, tennis ball–sized husks when they're soft enough to make a dent with your thumb. A few black spots on the husk are fine, but leave behind any husks that are mostly black.

Always handle black walnut husks with gloves

On the tree, ripe black walnuts look like tennis balls.

The large, spreading form of a mature black walnut makes it an attractive shade tree.

on. They are a traditional dye source and will stain your fingers a brownish yellow that lasts for weeks. There are several ways to remove the husks, which are tenacious. I put on an old pair of boots and stomp on them to break the husk, then peel it off with gloved hands, dropping the nut in a large bucket of water. (Don't be alarmed by the maggots inhabiting the husk; they can't penetrate the nut's shell.) Next I scrub off remnants of the husks and get rid of any floaters. Floating nuts are hollow inside, never having developed good nutmeat.

Nuts must be cured before they can be used, so spread them out in a single layer in a shallow crate or on a screen (something

Even after black walnut husks decay, the hard-shelled nut inside remains edible.

that allows air to circulate around the nuts) and let them dry for two to four weeks. Do NOT leave the nuts unprotected outdoors, where squirrels will steal them overnight, laughing their high-pitched squirrel laughs and leaving only a few hollow, undeveloped nuts behind. Not that this happened to me . . .

The final step is shelling the nuts. Lest you think you're home free, remember that black walnut shells are

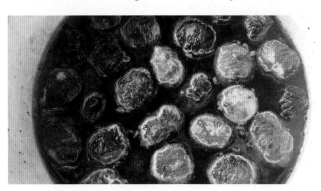

Once the husks are removed, clean the nuts before curing.

Good air circulation is crucial for curing the nuts.

considerably thicker than the shells of their English cousins. I place my nuts in a vise, slowly increasing pressure so the shell will break, leaving the nut as intact as possible. It's a slow process.

## HOW TO EAT IT

After all that work, I hope you like the taste of black walnuts. Some people do, and some people don't.

The flavor is stronger than that of English walnuts, heavier, darker, almost winelike. You can combine them with milder nuts in breads and pies, or feature them in cookies and ice cream.

Black walnuts have a high fat content and must be eaten or frozen soon after shelling. In their shells, they'll last a year or more.

Black walnuts are tough nuts to crack. Using a vise will help crack the shell while keeping the nut meat whole.

SPRING  SUMMER  FALL  WINTER

# CHESTNUT

*Castanea dentata*

**What it is:** a majestic deciduous tree
**Where to find it:** woods, yards
**Edible parts:** nuts

Beware the needle-like spines of the chestnut covering!

## THE DETAILS

Early in the twentieth century, a fungal disease attacked American chestnut trees in New York City and quickly spread among East Coast chestnut populations. Chestnut blight (as the fungus is called) doesn't kill the entire tree, but it does kill top growth. Trees may resprout from the roots and grow for several years before succumbing to the blight once again. Chestnut blight hasn't reached the West Coast, however, and American chestnuts grow well there. Settlers to the Pacific Northwest brought chestnuts with them in the nineteenth century, and today the oldest populations of the American chestnut tree can be found in that part of the country.

The Chinese chestnut (*C. mollissima*) and Japanese chestnut (*C. crenata*) are resistant to chestnut blight, but their fruits aren't as sweet as those of the American chestnut, nor are the trees as large and imposing in the landscape. Current breeding programs integrating a small amount of Asian chestnut DNA into the American chestnut genome offer the promise of producing blight-resistant American chestnuts. Chestnut trees (American and otherwise) grow best in full to part sun.

## HOW TO HARVEST

Watch your trees carefully; humans aren't the only animals who treasure ripe chestnuts. As fruit ripens in

Unripe chestnut casings are almost the same color as the foliage that surrounds them. Inside lies rich, brown, chestnutty goodness.

early to mid fall, the spiny outer casing opens to reveal the chestnuts within. This is the perfect time to harvest, while the open fruit is still on the tree. Shortly thereafter the fruit falls from the trees, and the early forager gets the chestnut. It may be you, it may be a squirrel, it may be a raccoon. I encourage you to be first in line.

Pack a pair of thick leather gloves, because those spines are sharp! This is no time to be macho. You'll harvest more nuts, faster, if you protect your hands. And you'll need those gloves when you're prying out the nuts, too. After the involucre (a fancy word for the afore-mentioned spiny casing) opens, it becomes flexible.

Wearing your gloves, you should be able to flex it backwards, enlarging the opening enough to pry or pop out the nuts. I've tried this without protection (in my lustful rush toward deliciousness). Nothing squelches your appetite like pain, so learn from my mistake.

Ripe chestnuts should be a rich brown color.

## LOOK-ALIKE TO AVOID

Horse chestnuts (left) and edible chestnuts (right) are not the same plant! Not only is the foliage quite different (horse chestnuts have palmate leaves, chestnuts have simple leaves), but the nut of the horse chestnut is bitter and toxic.

Occasionally unripe nuts, showing some green, will fall from the tree prematurely. Because chestnuts are more perishable than most nuts, they do not ripen well once they've fallen from the tree.

In addition to the blight mentioned above, chestnut lovers should be on the lookout for the chestnut maggot. A small hole in the shell indicates that a larva has crawled out of the nut and burrowed into the ground to overwinter. The good news is that the hole indicates the maggot has fled. The bad news is that a nut without a hole may or may not have a maggot inside. If you process the nuts immediately, look for bugs and remove them. If you don't have time to cook with your chestnuts right away, store them in the freezer, lest maggots exit the nuts onto your kitchen counter. When you thaw them, clean out any frozen insects, unless you crave the extra protein.

## HOW TO EAT IT

With a serrated knife make an X on the flat side of each nut. (The serrated knife gives you a better grip.) This allows steam to escape from the nuts and prevents them from exploding in the oven. Place the chestnuts on a cookie sheet and roast at 400°F for 25 minutes. You'll notice the skins start to peel back from the X. The shells and inner skin will come off easily when the nuts are still warm.

Roasted chestnuts are a classic stuffing ingredient. They also make a wonderful savory soup and a superb dessert soufflé. But I prefer to focus on the unique flavor and texture of the chestnut, eating it as plain as possible. Because chestnuts contain more starch than any other nut, they're often used in vegetable recipes. An excellent way to highlight the nuts' moist density is to serve them as a side dish, mixed with boiled potatoes and topped with a little butter or a super-light tomato sauce.

Foraged chestnuts are often smaller than store-bought, but they taste just as sweet!

Some people enjoy chestnuts raw. Allow them to mature for a few weeks after harvesting, to develop sweetness. Shell the nuts, then let them sit on the counter to ripen. You'll have to peel the outer covering before you eat the nut, which is more challenging to do with a raw nut than with a roasted one. The easiest way is to slice the nut in half, then carefully work the skin off with a sharp knife. The crunchy nut meat can be eaten plain or sliced into salads.

SPRING    SUMMER    FALL    WINTER

# GINKGO

*Ginkgo biloba*

**What it is:** a deciduous tree
**Where to find it:** yards, parks, city streets
**Edible parts:** seeds

## THE DETAILS

Ginkgos are most appreciated for their unusual leaf shape and brilliant yellow fall foliage. These trees are dioecious, meaning that trees are either male or female. Most gardeners prefer male trees, since female trees produce unbelievably stinky fruit. The flesh surrounding each ginkgo seed smells like cheesy vomit. (There, I said it.) But the nut is so delicious, it's definitely worth putting up with the smell.

Ginkgos have a characteristic narrow, upright shape. They grow best in full sun and a moist, well-drained soil. Some vendors market trees as female or male, but without DNA analysis it's difficult to determine the sex of a tree

Nothing else looks like a ginkgo leaf.

A large ginkgo is an impressive shade tree; they're often found in parks and along city streets.

When ginkgo foliage turns yellow, start looking beneath the trees for ripe fruit.

before it reaches bearing age, which can be about 10 years. If fruit is what you're after, you can also graft female branches onto male trees.

I was astonished to learn that the Urban Forestry Administration of the District of Columbia actually sprays female ginkgos with a growth inhibitor that prevents fruit development. If this doesn't satisfy smell-sensitive inhabitants, they will remove and replace female ginkgos if 60 percent of the neighborhood agrees. Cutting down a beautiful, mature tree that provides nutrition and deliciousness just because it smells bad for a few weeks in fall? Crime against nature, if you ask me.

### HOW TO HARVEST

Wait until the fruit (technically, a fleshy cone) falls to the ground in autumn. Wearing latex gloves, pick up the fruit and squeeze

> **Ginkgo nuts are popular ingredients in Far Eastern cuisines, and it's not unusual to find Asian women at botanical gardens and in city parks, gathering the seeds.**

the seed into a plastic bag, leaving the smelly flesh behind. Wash away any fleshy remnants clinging to the seeds, then process the nuts or freeze them in their shells for later use.

Ginkgo nuts are popular ingredients in Far Eastern cuisines, and it's not unusual to find Asian women at botanical gardens and in city parks, gathering the seeds. Foragers can be territorial and ginkgo fruit is generally abundant, so give people their space.

## HOW TO EAT IT

Let me count the ways. Ginkgo nuts should only be eaten cooked, not raw (they taste terrible). I bake them at 300°F for about an hour, then shell them. Use a hammer or a rubber mallet to crack the shells between layers of dish towels to avoid smashing the nut meats. Rub off any papery skins that don't come off with the shells.

Cooked nuts turn emerald green, adding both visual and gustatory interest to soups, rice, and noodle dishes. To best appreciate the taste and dense texture of ginkgo nuts, fry them in oil and sprinkle with salt. These make an excellent snack with beer, sake, or wine. Ginkgo nuts are also used in traditional Asian desserts. In sweet recipes, uncooked nuts are shelled, then cooked (usually boiled) before being added to puddings, cakes, and sweet soups.

White shells contain brown nuts that turn green when fried.

# OAK

## *Quercus* species

**What it is:** a large deciduous tree
**Where to find it:** yards, parks, roadsides, woods
**Edible parts:** nuts

> Acorns can be ground into flour and used in baked goods, or coarsely ground and used as nuts in cookies and breads. They also make a fantastic soup, hearty and thick on a cold autumn evening.

A single oak this size can provide all the acorns you'll want.

## THE DETAILS

Everyone knows the oak tree. Its characteristic lobed leaves make it easy to identify, at least to the genus level. After that, things get tricky. White oaks have a reputation for the tastiest acorns. Their leaves are generally softly lobed, with rounded edges. Red oaks require more work to make them palatable. They contain more tannins, and their lobed leaves are pointier and sharper. In fact, the California or coast live oak (*Quercus agrifolia,* a species of red oak) is downright prickly. Its leaf looks more like a holly leaf, but its long acorn is unmistakably oak.

What no one talks about is that oak trees interbreed very freely. I'm not saying they're promiscuous, but the resulting naturally occurring hybrids can be hard to differentiate. Oaks grow best in full sun and well-drained soil.

## HOW TO HARVEST

I don't bother to identify the species when harvesting acorns. Sue me. I think the size of the nut is more important than whether the tree is a red oak or a white oak. Large nuts mean less work per ounce of usable nut meat. Less work is good.

Collect acorns as soon as they fall. Acorns left on the ground are susceptible to penetration by insects, making them unfit for human consumption. Once collected, acorns can be frozen until you have time to work with them.

Acorns must be shelled before they can be processed. The shell is relatively thin and easy to crack with a hammer. Place several nuts between layers of a dish towel and smack them, then pick the meats out of the shells.

Harvest your acorns as soon as possible to reduce the likelihood of insects ruining your crop.

There are many different ways to process acorns; all involve leaching the nuts of their bitter-tasting tannins. I prefer to leach them, then store the nuts in the refrigerator or freezer, grinding as needed. Storing the nutmeats in large pieces keeps them fresher because the decreased surface area results in slower oxidation.

Hot leaching (boiling the nuts in progressive changes of water until the bitter taste is gone) is fast. If you plan to use your acorns as nuts, this is a good way to go. Don't rely on the color of the water to tell you when your acorns are done. Instead, taste a nut. It may take anywhere from three to many more changes of water to leach out the bitter taste.

The end product of hot leaching does not bind well as a flour once it's been heated beyond 150°F. If your aim is to make acorn flour, cold leaching is the way to go. And short of anchoring a bag of shelled acorns in a quickly flowing stream (which is just what the laughing squirrels hope you'll do), the easiest way to cold-leach those nuts is to stash them in the back of your toilet. (I'll wait while you read that sentence again because yes, I'm serious, in the back of your toilet.)

To be clear: I'm talking about the toilet TANK, not the toilet bowl. Empty the toilet tank and scrub it out, then refill it (with perfectly clean, drinkable water), put your shelled acorns in a jelly bag, and drop the bag into a clean toilet tank. Each flush washes cold water through the nut meats, leaching them of their bitterness. Taste-test at intervals after 24 hours. You may need as long as two to three days.

Either way you leach them, dry the acorns (dehydrate at 125°F for 12 to 16 hours) and remove the *testa* (papery covering) before using them. Hot processing removes the testas, but cold-processed acorns will need to be peeled by hand after they've dried.

## HOW TO EAT IT

Cold-leached acorns can be ground into flour and used in baked goods, substituting for up to half the amount of regular flour. Because it contains no gluten, acorn flour won't bind and rise. My favorite baked acorn flour recipe is a take on New England brown bread, baked in a bean can (see acorn brown bread recipe on page 220).

Hot-leached acorns can be coarsely ground and used as nuts in cookies and breads. They also make a fantastic soup, hearty and thick on a cold autumn evening.

# PIÑON PINE

## *Pinus edulis*

**What it is:** a needle evergreen tree
**Where to find it:** southwestern United States
**Edible parts:** seeds

## THE DETAILS

While all pine nuts (technically seeds) are edible, only a few pine species produce seeds that are big enough and tasty enough to make collecting them worthwhile. Bringing in the pine nut harvest is a lot of work. Once you've done it, you'll never grumble at the high cost of pine nuts in the grocery store again. Still, it's worth gathering your own if only for bragging rights . . . and the chance to taste truly fresh pine nuts.

Pine nuts take two seasons to mature, and crop size varies greatly from year to year and place to place. Although piñon pines are drought-tolerant trees, extreme dryness impairs the development of seeds.

Seeds that feel lighter than others or that have a light color may have aborted in their shells. Darker-colored seeds are probably heavy and full.

Piñon pines grow best in full sun and quick-draining soil. A related species, *Pinus monophylla* produces a similar tasty seed, but its needles are held singly, instead of in pairs. *Pinus koraiensis* is another cold-hardy pine (Zone 4) that produces an edible nut; the taste is slightly less strong than that of American pine nuts.

## HOW TO HARVEST

There are two ways to harvest pine nuts. If the pine cones have already opened, spread a tarp beneath the tree and shake the trunk, dislodging the seeds from between the

These piñon pines are full of cones, but are the cones full of nuts?

These pine nuts are ready to be harvested.

scales on each cone. Or, you can collect the cones and shake the seeds out in the comfort of your own kitchen.

If the pine cones are full-size (compare them to open cones on the same tree) but haven't opened, you can hurry them along in one of two ways. Roasting the cones will cause the scales to open, freeing the seeds. Spread them on a cookie sheet and bake at 350°F until you see the cones open. A somewhat slower (but also easier) method is to keep the cones in a paper bag and allow them to dry over several weeks. Once they have dried, the scales open; shake the bag to free the nuts from inside the cones.

## HOW TO EAT IT

Each individual seed has a thin shell that must be cracked and removed. It's easy to break the nut in the process, so be gentle. You won't need a hammer to crack the shell. Place the nuts between layers of a dish towel and press on them with the bottom of a thick drinking glass until you hear a crack. Pine nuts are tasty raw or toasted. To toast them, spread a single layer on a cookie sheet and bake at 350°F for about 10 minutes. Use nuts in pestos, in cookies, on top of salads, or as a superior snack.

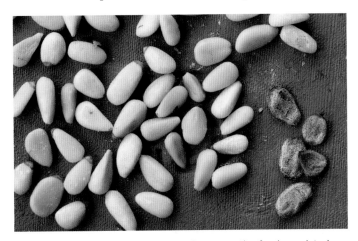

Note the difference in appearance between the fresh, moist pine nuts (left) and the dried, shriveled nuts (right). The dried nuts were either harvested late or didn't get enough moisture during development. They aren't worth eating.

# CHAPTER 6

# HIDDEN TREASURE:
# Roots, Tubers, and Rhizomes

I'd rather have this fragrant bouquet of wild garlic bulbs than a bunch of flowers.

# Underground plant parts offer surprising rewards.

Some, like wild onion, wild garlic, and wild ginger, have strong, spicy flavors. Others are rich in carbohydrates and contain significant amounts of protein and fiber. Some rank lower on the glycemic index than traditional tubers like potatoes and yams, making them healthy choices when compared to other carbs.

Plants with underground storage tissue in the form of corms, tubers, and bulbs are categorized as geophytes. Most geophytes should be harvested in early spring or late fall, when plants are not in active growth and the underground parts of the plant are full of stored nutrition. During active growth, plants draw on that nutrition, so the storage tissue will be smaller and less nourishing. When they are properly harvested, you can eat these geophytes without sacrificing the beauty and vigor of their aboveground parts.

## CANNA

### *Canna edulis* and *C. indica*

**What it is:** a sun-loving tender perennial
**Where to find it:** gardens
**Edible parts:** rhizomes

### THE DETAILS

This beloved garden plant is probably not something you'll find growing in the wild, but if you're growing cannas and they've thrived and multiplied, you might try eating a rhizome or two. Canna rhizomes are fibrous, containing large grains, which can be separated from the fibers to produce an easily digestible starch that can be used like arrowroot. In South America, cannas are a traditional agricultural crop, and the starch in *Canna edulis* (a.k.a. *C. discolor*) is ground into flour. In Vietnam, the starch is used to make cellophane noodles.

As a garden plant, ornamental cultivars are grown for their beauty rather than for their culinary value. Many have extraordinary variegated foliage and showy blooms. The rhizomes of these highly ornamental varieties are less easy to cook with and more densely fibrous than those of *C. edulis*, which has plain green leaves and red flowers.

Cannas grow best in full sun and do well in containers. They are versatile ornamentals, growing equally well in water or in soil. If you grow them as aquatic plants, start the roots growing in soil first,

The tubers of *Canna edulis* are less fibrous and easier to cook with than most other canna rhizomes.

and transfer the plants to your water garden after leaves have appeared.

## HOW TO HARVEST

Once again, a single task can accomplish two goals: harvesting and garden maintenance. Since cannas aren't frost hardy, many gardeners have to dig them up to overwinter the plants. Why not take a few into the kitchen at the same time? When the foliage has died back, dig up your cannas and save aside the youngest (most tender) rhizomes for cooking. Keep the rest in a dark, frost-free location until it's time to plant them outside the following spring.

## HOW TO EAT IT

Canna rhizomes taste like potatoes, much more so than Jerusalem artichokes or hopniss tubers do. I've cooked them low and long (6 hours at 250°F) and high and fast (1 hour at 450°F). I've baked them, both peeled and unpeeled. I've cut them into chunks and soaked them before baking. I've boiled them and then baked them. In every instance, the outer layer remains very fibrous and I've ended up scooping out the center of the rhizome to eat. Mashed with a little butter, you might not realize it wasn't a traditional spud, except that the flesh turns brownish with baking.

If you're feeling adventurous, try making canna starch by grating the rhizome into water, then stirring it around.

Pour the mixture through a layer of cheesecloth or a yogurt strainer to remove the fibers, then let the starch settle out of the reserved water. Pour off the water, leaving the starch at the bottom of your container, then refill with water, stir it around, and allow the starch to settle a second time. Pour off the water again and use the remaining starch to thicken fruit sauces or make pudding. If you're going to use the starch right away, you can use it wet. If you'd like to save for future use, dry it in a dehydrator before storing.

Peel away the fibrous outer layer of canna rhizomes to enjoy their soft, potato-y insides.

Don't expect to make vats of pudding with your canna starch; a cup of grated canna roots makes about 1½ teaspoons of starch. (Commercial operations are far more efficient.)

> Canna rhizomes taste like potatoes, much more so than Jerusalem artichokes or hopniss tubers do.

SPRING   SUMMER   FALL   WINTER

# DAHLIA

## *Dahlia* species

**What it is:** a sun-loving tender perennial
**Where to find it:** gardens
**Edible parts:** tubers

> I find raw tubers reminiscent of radishes and like them thinly sliced or grated in salads or coleslaw.

## THE DETAILS

Dahlias come in many sizes, colors, and FLAVORS! This old-fashioned garden plant grows best in full sun and rich, well-drained soils. They perform well in containers. While dahlia flowers have been used for years as a garnish, their petals don't actually have much taste. Dahlia tubers, however, are a traditional food in Central America. Written sources dating back as far as the sixteenth century describe it as an edible tuber, and dahlia tubers are still a featured ingredient in Oaxacan cuisine. Additionally, a hot beverage (called *dacopa*) is made from powdered, roasted dahlia tubers and is enjoyed both for its own taste and as a coffee substitute. Dahlia tubers have a range of tastes,

You can grow your dahlias and eat them, too.

depending on the plant. Taste a sliver of the raw root before cooking with it.

Like many edible members of the daisy family, dahlias store nutrition in the form of inulin in their roots and tubers. Inulin is considered healthy for several reasons: It's a good source of fiber, it increases calcium absorption, and — unlike the starch in potatoes and other traditional root vegetables — it doesn't raise blood sugar or triglyceride levels because it isn't readily digestible by humans. If not fully cooked, inulin may cause flatulence when consumed in large quantities. To gauge how your body will react, start with a small portion.

It's not unusual for a dahlia tuber to start growing before it's replanted in spring.

## HOW TO HARVEST

Dahlias are not frost hardy, so many gardeners dig them up for winter storage. As soon as frost has killed your dahlias' top growth, dig their tubers and clean them, by brushing off any clumps of dirt that cling to them. Those you plan to replant in spring should be allowed to dry, then stored in peat moss or sand over the winter. Choose the youngest, plumpest tubers to bring back to the kitchen.

## HOW TO EAT IT

Peel your dahlia tubers and try a thin slice to get a handle on the taste. I find raw tubers reminiscent of radishes and like them thinly sliced or grated in salads or coleslaw. Remember that raw inulin may cause flatulence in some people, although a few slices of tuber added to a salad is a small enough amount that it shouldn't be problematic for most. The grated flesh can also be used like zucchini to make quick bread (see page 219). Dahlia tubers can be boiled, roasted, or baked, but cooked tubers don't have a strong taste. Think of them as a blank canvas, waiting to receive your unique blend of herbs and spices.

SPRING  SUMMER  FALL  WINTER

# HOPNISS, GROUNDNUT

*Apios americana*

**What it is:** a perennial vine
**Where to find it:** gardens, lakesides and riverbanks
**Edible parts:** tubers

Chains of delicious hopniss tubers, freshly dug.

## THE DETAILS

This vine is a champion, and everyone should grow it! The flowers are gorgeous and highly fragrant. The vines grow rapidly, covering 15 to 25 feet in a single season, and their foliage is pinnate and attractive. Because the vines die back to the ground every fall, the plant is easier to control than its more aggressive and flashier (although distinctly non-delicious) cousin, wisteria. Hopniss grows best in full to part sun and a moist, well-drained soil. It does very well in containers.

The underground tubers are the tastiest edible part of the hopniss plant. They were an essential part of the Native American diet and contain three times as much protein as potatoes, based on dry weight. In warmer climates the plant produces beans, but my growing season is too short to produce a substantial harvest. I've been able to cook a few, and while the taste was good, the beans themselves were too fibrous

The leaves and vines of hopniss resemble those of wisteria.

Hopniss blooms are so fragrant, I often smell them before I see the flowers.

From top to bottom: cleaned tubers, peeled and sliced tubers, roasted tubers.

to be pleasant. Perhaps a longer or different method of cooking would work, or perhaps the shelled inner beans would be a better food choice. Sadly I've never had a big enough harvest to experiment further.

## HOW TO HARVEST

It just keeps getting better. Harvesting edible tubers also rejuvenates the plant, combining two tasks into one. Who doesn't like that? So, while tubers can be harvested throughout the year, why not combine your collecting with putting the garden to bed for winter? Once foliage dies back, cut the vines to about 6 inches above the ground. Next, dig into the soil around the crowns of each vine and you'll uncover chains of tubers ranging from the size of an almond to the size of a tennis ball.

Tubers should be allowed to grow for two to three years before collecting an edible crop. After that, you may harvest a third to half of the tubers each year, replanting any that

> The underground tubers are the tastiest edible part of the hopniss plant. They were an essential part of the Native American diet and contain three times as much protein as potatoes.

are too small to eat. I don't keep anything smaller than a peach pit. Wash and dry the tubers, trimming away the chains and small roots. Hopniss lasts in the refrigerator or root cellar for several months.

## HOW TO EAT IT

Young tubers (up to about the size of a golf ball) don't need to be peeled, although you certainly may peel them if you like. Older tubers, with thicker, darker skins, should be peeled before cooking. There are as many ways to cook hopniss tubers as there are to cook potatoes. Since the flavor of hopniss is so superb, I suggest skipping the heavy cream and cheese sauces to focus on the tuber's nutty deliciousness.

Small tubers can be eaten whole; larger tubers can be sliced ¼ to ½ inch thick. Toss them in olive oil, salt, and pepper and roast in a 400°F oven until they're easily pierceable with a fork. Or parboil for a few minutes, then sauté in butter. The taste is like a nutty potato. Once you've tried it, you'll crave more.

SPRING   SUMMER   FALL   WINTER

# JERUSALEM ARTICHOKE, SUNCHOKE, J-CHOKE

*Helianthus tuberosus*

**What it is:** a sun-loving perennial
**Where to find it:** gardens, parks, roadsides
**Edible parts:** tubers

## THE DETAILS

Neither an artichoke nor from Jerusalem, these sunflowers are the perfect combination of ornamental and edible. Growing from 4 to 10 feet tall (depending on growing conditions and cultivars), J-chokes have classic yellow daisy flowers and unusually tasty tuberous roots. Two characteristics make them easy to identify: 1) The center of the flower is yellow, not black or brown, and 2) the leaves feel like sandpaper and are joined to the stem by winged petioles.

It's now possible to find the tubers for sale in supermarkets, but why

Left to their own devices, J-chokes spread rapidly in a sunny location.

not grow your own? This perennial crop grows quickly enough to provide both an annual harvest and enough tubers to replant for next year's bloom. It's drought tolerant once established and grows well in containers.

## HOW TO HARVEST

Jerusalem artichokes should be divided and harvested regularly. They'll grow better that way, and it will also prevent them from taking over your garden. These plants can be aggressive. Dig up your tubers in fall, preferably after the first frost or two, and feel free to keep at least half for cooking before you replant the remainder. The flowers will be long past, so you won't be sacrificing bloom.

J-chokes can be harvested from fall to spring, at which time the plants will start drawing on the nutrition reserves

> Dig up your tubers in fall, preferably after the first frost or two, and feel free to keep at least half for cooking before you replant the remainder.

stored in the tuber. They keep for a few weeks in the refrigerator, or you can leave them in the ground until you're ready to eat

The leaves of Jerusalem artichokes have an unusual winged petiole, which can help you identify the plant. A petiole is the stem that connects the leaf to the main plant stem; the J-choke's petiole has a wing of leaf tissue on either side of the petiole itself.

More than just a pretty face: the yellow center of the Jerusalem artichoke is a key identifying characteristic.

them. It's important not to harvest J-chokes before they ripen in fall or their starch (inulin) may cause flatulence. Thorough cooking removes this danger.

Garden-grown Jerusalem artichoke tubers may look slightly different from store-bought. Tubers cultivated as an edible crop tend to be round, while tubers grown in nonagricultural soils may be longer and thinner. The taste is the same, though, and the tubers can be used in the same way.

## HOW TO EAT IT

People who expect the tubers to be a potato substitute will be disappointed. Not because the flavor is in any way inferior (it isn't), but because the texture of a J-choke will never be light and fluffy. So use it in ways that highlight its unique virtues, rather than try to make it conform to an unrealistic standard.

Fully ripe Jerusalem artichokes are sweet and crisp when raw; slice them thinly into salads or add sunchoke matchsticks to a tray of crudités. When baked, they become sweet and almost liquid inside. J-chokes can also be boiled, roasted, or sautéed. Try peeling them, boiling in milk, then blending to make a smooth purée. Add a little butter, some salt and pepper, and you have a side dish fit for a queen. Or use them instead of potatoes for a new take on vichyssoise or sunchoke leek soup.

Can you tell if this tuber is store-bought or wild grown?

# LOTUS

## *Nelumbo nucifera* and *N. lutea*

**What it is:** a perennial aquatic plant
**Where to find it:** water gardens, lakes, ponds
**Edible parts:** roots, nuts, leaves, flower petals

## THE DETAILS

Lotuses are large, impressive aquatic plants that grow best in full sun. They have showy flowers in pink, white, or yellow (depending on the species), sculptural seed heads, and large leaves that may either float on the water's surface or stand 3 to 5 feet above the water, depending on the depth of the water. These are not water lilies! Water lilies belong to a completely different genus, *Nymphaea.*

The Chinese lotus (*N. nucifera*) and the native American lotus (*N. lutea*) can be used in the same ways, both in the garden and in the kitchen. Many parts of the plant are edible: the ripe nuts, young leaves, flower petals, and tuberous roots. The roots are my favorite part. They make a

Lotus leaves, seed pods, and flowers are all highly ornamental, not to mention edible.

tasty and beautiful dish, especially if you feature the intricate pattern of holes that run lengthwise through the root.

## HOW TO HARVEST

Unlike many tubers, which can be harvested anytime between fall and spring, lotus roots should be harvested from late

summer through mid fall. Earlier in the season immature tubers will be small, and later they'll be tough and fibrous. Tubers grow linked together, looking like a string of sausages.

Lotus tubers grow buried in mud at the bottom of ponds. If yours are in containers, harvesting is

relatively easy. In a pond, you may have to dig down as far as a foot to reach the tubers. Cut between the linked tubers to remove those you want for cooking and replant the rest.

## HOW TO EAT IT

Wash the lotus root, slice off each end, and look through the hollow tubes to make sure they're clean. If there's mud inside, rinse it out. Then, use a vegetable peeler to remove the skin and reveal the white flesh of the root.

No matter how you cook lotus, it will always retain a little bit of crunch, even after 10 hours in a slow cooker. Use it in stir-fries, soups, or stews, or deep-fry slices as chips. While I don't often choose deep-frying as my preferred method of cooking, some foods cry out for the Fry Daddy . . . and lotus root is one of them. Slice it thinly with a mandolin and toss the slices in the hot, hot oil. Add a sprinkle of salt to the finished chips, which are crisp, tasty, and very pretty to look at.

While several aboveground parts of the lotus are also edible, the roots (shown here sliced and fried) are my favorite crop.

## LOOK-ALIKE TO AVOID

The casual observer may confuse the lotus with the water lily (pictured). The flowers and foliage of water lilies float on the water's surface, whereas the flowers and foliage of lotus often stand above the water, depending on its depth. Additionally, water lily foliage shows a radial slit or cutout. While water lilies have edible parts, they require different preparation than the lotus.

SPRING    SUMMER    FALL    WINTER

# WILD GARLIC

## *Allium vineale*

**What it is:** a perennial vegetable
**Where to find it:** fields, yards, roadsides
**Edible parts:** bulbs, leaves, flowers, bulbils

The best time to harvest whole plants of wild garlic and wild onion is in spring or fall, when the bulbs are plump and full. The leaves can be snipped for use as an herb anytime during the year.

Unlike cultivated garlic, wild garlic foliage is hollow inside.

## THE DETAILS

Despite its name, wild garlic resembles the traditional onion more than garlic in both taste and appearance. It grows to be 12 to 18 inches tall with hollow gray-green leaves emerging from a single bulb between 1 and 2 centimeters in diameter. Flowers are followed by small bulbils (small bulbs), which can be propagated to make more plants. *Allium canadense* (a.k.a. wild onion) is a close relative, but has solid leaves and a distinctive netted sheath covering the bulb. Both smell intensely like garlic or onions and are equally useful in the kitchen. All alliums are edible, although some are tastier than others. The most famous wild onion is *Allium tricoccum*, also known as ramps. It's a woodland delicacy that has unfortunately been overharvested in the wild. Of course you could always plant ramps in your backyard and harvest guilt-free! They grow best in full to part sun.

## HOW TO HARVEST

To harvest the underground bulbs, grasp the stem a few inches above its crown and pull straight up. The entire root system should come up easily. Collecting wild garlic means reducing the plant population, so bear this in mind when harvesting and leave some behind for next year. While wild garlic does not have classic garlic-type cloves, it may produce a few small bulbs alongside the main bulb. The best time to harvest wild garlic and wild onion is in spring or fall, when the bulbs are plump and full.

The leaves of wild garlic and wild onion can be

These cleaned garlic bulbs can be used fresh or preserved by drying.

snipped for use as an herb anytime during the year. Blooms are also edible. Individual flowers are often followed by bulbils, and sometimes bulbils grow instead of flowers. These bulbils may sprout, fall off, and take root. Toss a few on the ground to propagate the species, and take the rest home to cook with.

## HOW TO EAT IT

Wild allium bulbs make a strong and delicious onion substitute. Some people consider wild garlic to be too strong, but I disagree.

The bulbs have a slightly tougher texture than traditional onions do, and a hearty taste that combines perfectly with wild, bitter greens. You can use them fresh, or dry them for future use. Either way, taste one before you use them; not everyone appreciates their robust flavor.

The foliage of wild garlic can be snipped and used like chives. Flowers can be added to salads. Round, green bulbils make a tasty pickle, or you can chop them up and use them like the bulbs.

SPRING　SUMMER　FALL　WINTER

# WILD GINGER

*Asarum canadense*

**What it is:** a shade-loving deciduous ground cover
**Where to find it:** gardens, woods
**Edible parts:** rhizomes

## THE DETAILS

The demure, heart-shaped leaves of our native ginger have a matte finish and lack the showy white venation of their European cousins. I prefer the native, both for its taste and the medium green, textured backdrop it provides for its garden companions. This plant spreads steadily but slowly. If you look beneath its leaves in late spring, you may glimpse its unusual flowers. They grow on the soil's surface and are pollinated by flies and beetles. Wild ginger grows in mixed deciduous woods, in dappled to dense shade. It tolerates both dry and moist soils and grows well among rocks. You'll often find it alongside trilliums (*Trillium* species), foamflowers (*Tiarella* species), and Christmas fern (*Polystichum acrostichoides*) among oak and beech trees.

The heart-shaped leaves of wild ginger make an excellent low-growing groundcover. Peek beneath them to discover their unusual flowers growing on the soil's surface.

## HOW TO HARVEST

Wild ginger rhizomes connect plants underground and grow at a depth of 1 inch to several inches. They should be harvested in late fall, when the plants are entering dormancy. Since the leaves are evergreen in many locations, don't wait for them to die back.

Gently dig up several clumps of ginger, noticing how they're linked by the rhizome. This is the spicy, edible part of the plant. Make a cut near the base of each plant, severing the connecting rhizome but leaving some roots on each plant. Then replant the clumps of ginger. Wash the rhizomes and roots. These can be used fresh, or dehydrated and stored for later use.

## HOW TO EAT IT

Wild ginger combines well with both savory and sweet tastes. The flavor isn't exactly like that of tropical ginger; it's even more delicious, with a darker, more complex taste. It has haunted me since I first tried it. Finely chopped or ground in a spice grinder, the fresh or dried rhizomes can be substituted for traditional ginger or used with spicebush berries instead of cinnamon and nutmeg. Use wild ginger to flavor pear and apple pies and crisps, or in a marinade for chicken, pork, or fish. Once you've tried wild ginger, its unique taste will inspire creativity in your kitchen.

Only the rhizomes of wild ginger are edible, not the foliage.

# CHAPTER 7

# SUPERSTARS:
# Plants with Many Edible Parts

Daylily petals can be used to color a bowl of rice or pasta.

## If a plant has three or more edible parts

I think it deserves special consideration. And so I present my superstars, four garden inhabitants that offer superior ingredients throughout the growing season.

SPRING  SUMMER  FALL  WINTER

# DANDELION

## Taraxacum officinale

**What it is:** a perennial weed
**Where to find it:** gardens, parks, fields
**Edible parts:** leaves, flower buds, flower petals, roots

## THE DETAILS

Does anyone *not* recognize the dandelion? I didn't think so. A ubiquitous denizen of sunny lawns, fields, and playgrounds, the dandelion elicits strong feelings. If its toothed leaves and fluffy yellow flowers are the bane of your existence, I'm about to suggest an excellent revenge. Or if, like me, you don't care what plants make up your lawn as long as they're soft underfoot, then here's how you can enjoy one of the most versatile weeds around.

## HOW TO HARVEST

Dandelion greens are exceptionally nutritious, containing high levels of vitamin A, calcium, and potassium. They're tastiest in early spring, before they flower. As summer continues, leaves develop

These plump flowers are ready to harvest.

a bitter taste, although plants in shade may remain palatable. Grasp the rosette of foliage at its base, as close to the ground as possible. Twist and pull.

Unopened flower buds may be fried, boiled, or pickled. Once flowers have opened, the petals can be plucked to use in any number of ways. To separate the petals from the bitter green calyx at the flower's base, grab

Separate dandelion petals from their bitter-tasting calyx.

the base of the petals in one hand, the calyx in the other, and twist in opposite directions.

Dandelion petals make a delicious summer wine.

To make sure you get the entire tap root, dig dandelions with a long-bladed shovel.

Dandelions have taproots that are best harvested in late fall to early spring. Remember that a piece left behind will produce more flowers. If you'd like to cultivate your dandelion crop, this isn't a problem, but if you're trying to eliminate dandelions, remove the entire root.

## HOW TO EAT IT

Dandelion greens are packed with vitamins and minerals. I won't lie to you — they're bitter. But fresh young dandelion leaves are a good kind of bitter, the kind that gets your digestive juices flowing. They can be used raw in salads to balance mild greens like chickweed or miner's lettuce. Taste a leaf before you pick a bunch. Dandelion foliage can go from pleasantly bitter to overpowering in just a few days. Cooking the leaves gets rid of some bitterness and extends their useful season. Blanch them in boiling water, then use them in hortopita (see recipe on page 221), or egg dishes, or simply sauté them with olive oil and top with a squeeze of lemon juice.

Whole dandelion buds should be rinsed, then lightly boiled for no more than a minute or two. A little butter, some salt and pepper, and you're all set.

It takes 6 cups of dandelion petals to make a gallon of wine. That may not sound like a lot . . . until you start picking dandelion flowers and twisting off the petals. Petals have much less bulk than intact flowers do, and I usually need several days to collect enough for a batch of wine. If that seems daunting to you, add a cup of petals to oatmeal cookies in place of raisins, or to a loaf of savory bread, for a splash of color and texture.

While large roots can be eaten as a vegetable, their taste is mild and not particularly interesting. Instead, why not make your own version of New Orleans–style coffee by using roasted dandelion roots? Spread them out to dry for a few days, or dehydrate them in your dehydrator. Then roast the

These dandelion greens are tender and young, with just the right degree of bitterness; they're perfect for eating raw in a salad.

dry roots in a 350°F oven until the exterior of the roots is the color of your preferred coffee roast. This will take anywhere from 30 to 60 minutes. Let the roots cool, and then grind them to a powder. Pour 8 ounces of boiling water onto 1 tablespoon of the powder and let it steep for 5 minutes, then strain. The result is halfway between coffee and tea, and it's an excellent beverage with either milk or lemon.

SPRING  SUMMER  FALL  WINTER

# DAYLILY

*Hemerocallis fulva*

**What it is:** a perennial plant
**Where to find it:** gardens, roadsides
**Edible parts:** shoots, flower buds, flower petals, tubers

These unopened buds are all at the perfect stage for eating.

## THE DETAILS

Daylilies may be the most popular garden perennials ever. Numerous clubs and societies are devoted to the plant, but most members only appreciate the daylily for its looks, not its gustatory potential. There are thousands of daylily cultivars, and while some of them may be edible, my comments here describe the common orange-flowered species. Also, I have read a few reports of people having allergic reactions to eating daylilies. I know of many more people allergic to seafood and strawberries, but if this is your first time eating daylilies, start small.

Daylilies benefit from division every few years, so when it's time to divide, why not keep out a few pieces for the kitchen? And

These young shoots are tender and mild.

if you don't want to dig up your own, take a walk around the neighborhood. Over time, daylilies have outgrown their garden boundaries, so it's not unusual to find masses of this underappreciated edible plant growing wild in fields and along roadsides. Show the daylily some culinary love.

## HOW TO HARVEST

As the name indicates, the flowers of daylily last for a day. After the bloom opens, but before it starts to fade, pick a few flowers and remove the pistils and stamens (the interior parts). The petals can be used individually or as a whole. Unopened buds can be harvested from the time they're an inch long and entirely green, up until they're 3 inches long and showing color.

Collect young shoots until they're about 5 inches long; after that they tend to be fibrous. Snip them off right above the ground.

In fall or early spring, daylily tubers are plump and full of stored starches. Dig up a clump (or two) and remove up to two-thirds of the tubers, then replant the daylily. Clip the root hairs off the tubers, then clean them well. You'll probably need to wash them in several changes of water.

## HOW TO EAT IT

Mature daylily petals can be used dry or fresh. Crumble dry petals into rice or pasta to impart an orange-yellow color. Fresh petals add color to salads and, when kept whole (petals attached), make creative vessels for ice cream.

In Chinese cuisine daylily buds are an ingredient in classic hot and sour soup. You can add them raw to salads, where the crunch and taste are reminiscent of green beans. My favorite way to eat daylily buds is lightly sautéed in olive oil with salt and pepper.

Daylily shoots make a crisp spring vegetable. If

Cook daylily tubers as you would fingerling potatoes.

Drying intensifies the color of mature daylily petals.

you believe the accounts that describe their taste as scallion-like, you'll be disappointed. They are mild and crunchy but not particularly oniony. Still, they make a fresh side dish when lightly sautéed in olive oil or butter.

I've saved the best for last. Daylily tubers are mini potatoes. Why doesn't everybody know this? Yes, they're small, but no smaller than baby fingerlings. During the growing season, the tubers aren't substantial enough to be worth harvesting. Besides, the plant needs the nutrition stored in the tubers. But in fall and early spring, when these underground storage units are chock-full of starchy goodness, they are plump, delicate, and delicious. Coat them in olive oil, salt, and pepper, then roast at 450°F. You'll never look at a daylily in quite the same way again.

These daylily tubers are washed and ready for the roasting pan.

Buds can be eaten raw or cooked.

# MILKWEED

## *Asclepias syriaca*

**What it is:** a perennial plant or weed, depending on your point of view
**Where to find it:** gardens, roadsides
**Edible parts:** shoots, flower buds, flowers, young seedpods

The top 6 to 8 inches of these young milkweed stems are tender and tasty. Be sure to remove the leaves before cooking; they can impart a bitter taste.

## THE DETAILS

The common milkweed is a roadside weed for some people, but it has won the hearts of gardeners because of its plentiful, fragrant, and showy flowers. It's an essential food for Monarch butterfly larvae, and bees and butterflies are enthusiastic drinkers of milkweed nectar. Milkweed grows best in full sun and well-drained soil and is quite drought tolerant. It spreads by seed as well as by underground runners,

> If I had to choose just one plant to eat, it would be milkweed. It's delicious, plentiful, versatile, and lovely to look at.

and it can be an aggressive plant if left to its own devices. I occasionally yank up unwanted shoots in my yard, but I'm usually happy to have more milkweed within harvesting distance.

## HOW TO HARVEST

Young milkweed stems can be harvested when they're 6 to 8 inches tall. A quick tug at the base of the shoot is usually enough to snap it off, no pruners required. But wear gloves, because raw milkweed oozes a milky latex when cut or broken. It dries to a sticky mess. Sometimes the top 8 inches of older stems are tender enough to eat. If you can snap off the top of the stem with your hand, go ahead and gather.

The young flower buds of milkweed can be picked when they're tightly clustered, entirely green, and no bigger than a golf ball. Often they will be bracketed by two immature leaves, which are fine to include in your harvest.

Milkweed flowers should be gathered when they are fresh and full of

These milkweed flower buds are at the perfect stage to be harvested, blanched, sautéed, and devoured.

nectar. The nectar is often visible as clear drops of sticky (sugary!) liquid on the face of each flower. Be sure not to include any insect hitchhikers with your harvest.

Immature milkweed seedpods can be collected until they're about 1½ inches long. They should feel plump and firm, and the interiors should be entirely white. Open one up and take a look. If

there's any sign of brown developing, the pod is too mature for harvesting.

## HOW TO EAT IT

There are a lot of misconceptions about milkweed passed around in books and online. Some people claim it's bitter; others say it's downright poisonous. Correctly harvested and prepared, it is neither. In fact, if I had to choose just one plant to eat, it would

Mature flowers are best used in syrups, making the most of their tasty, sweet nectar.

be milkweed. Delicious, plentiful, versatile, and lovely to look at.

Here's what you need to know. No milkweed parts should be eaten raw. The shoots, flower buds, and pods of milkweed should be boiled, or blanched and then cooked to completion in a second way. It's not necessary to boil in three changes of water, as some people believe. However, cooking in water takes away the milky latex (not pleasant to eat), which is why I recommend blanching, even if you choose to cook the milkweed in a different way.

I believe the reports of milkweed's bitterness are most likely the result of people confusing it with dogbane (*Apocynum cannabinum*), a bitter, nonedible plant that superficially resembles milkweed but is actually pretty easy to differentiate. (Dogbane has red, branching, solid stems, while milkweed never branches and its stems are green and hollow.) Also, mature milkweed foliage can indeed be bitter and should be stripped from the young shoots before cooking. If cooked, the large leaves will impart their bitterness and obscure the taste of the milkweed stems, which would be a crying shame. It's fine to leave the last several pairs of immature leaves on the tip of the shoot.

The flavor of milkweed shoots most closely resembles that of green beans, only better. After a quick blanch, I toss them in olive oil and garlic, then roast them in a 450°F oven with a sprinkling of parmesan for about 15 minutes.

The flower buds may look like mini broccoli florets, but they are SO much tastier. Blanch them, then sauté in olive oil with salt and pepper.

Mature flowers can be dipped in batter and deep-fried as fritters, but then most of what you taste is batter and fat. I simmer the flowers in sugar and water, making a pink-purple simple syrup that can be frozen as a sorbet or mixed into cocktails. The taste is discernibly asclepiad to anyone familiar with the scent of a milkweed flower.

Immature milkweed pods are perfect for including in soups, stews, or vegetable stir-fries. Pods deliver the same green bean taste as the shoots and buds, but they stand up better to long cooking times, maintaining their shape and texture.

Milkweed freezes well, and all parts should be blanched before freezing. Thawed milkweed won't be crunchy, like the fresh stuff, but can be blended

Ripe seed pods should be picked when firm and smaller than 1 ½ inches long.

with stock to make a thick, savory soup.

## LOOK-ALIKE TO AVOID

Dogbane is related to common milkweed, but a close look makes it easy to tell the two plants apart. Dogbane flowers are white, while the flowers of common milkweed are pale pink. Both the flowers and the umbels (clusters) of dogbane flowers are significantly smaller than those of milkweed. Dogbane leaves are considerably narrower than milkweed leaves, and dogbane stems are red, branching, and solid, while milkweed stems are green, hollow, and never branching.

SPRING SUMMER FALL WINTER

## SASSAFRAS

*Sassafras albidum*

**What it is:** a deciduous tree
**Where to find it:** woods, roadsides
**Edible parts:** leaves, roots (root bark), and twigs

Green leaves can be picked any time before they start to turn color in fall. Sassafras twig syrup makes a delicious drink.

In the garden, sassafras offers multiple seasons of interest; here spring flowers are a fresh, bright green.

## THE DETAILS

Sassafras trees are native to North America. Theses medium-sized trees are valued in the landscape for their outstanding orange fall color and the fact that they produce three different leaf shapes on a single tree: oval, mitten-shaped, and three-lobed. Sassafras populations are clonal, with new trees emerging from an expanding underground root system. They aren't often found at nurseries or garden centers, which is a real shame. These are beautiful trees.

## HOW TO HARVEST

Green leaves can be picked anytime before they start to turn color in fall. Since they tend to form groves, you should have no trouble gathering enough leaves without noticeably defoliating the trees.

Young sassafras roots can be harvested by pulling up saplings from around the roots of the parent tree. Saplings smaller than 12 inches can usually be pulled up by hand, if you get a good

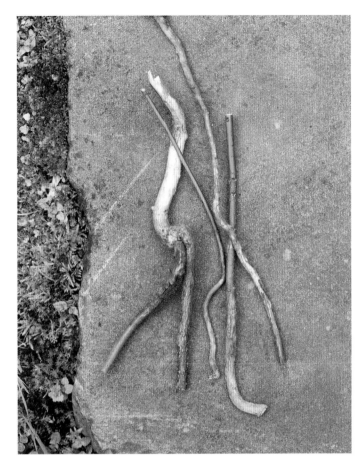

Small roots don't need to be peeled before boiling.

Glorious orange color indicates harvest time for these leaves has passed.

grip. Snip off the roots and wash them gently, discarding the top growth. Be sure not to scrape away the root bark, which is the source of most of the flavor.

Young twigs can be gathered year-round. They're easy to recognize in the winter landscape due to their characteristic green color and lemony smell. Scratch the bark to release the scent.

## HOW TO EAT IT

Dried sassafras leaves, ground fine and sieved to produce a powder, are the filé used in creole cooking, including gumbo. The powder is traditionally served in a bowl or shaker on the table, so people can add the amount they want. Stirred into the finished soup, filé thickens it with its mucilaginous properties.

Sassafras roots make a delicious and unique drink. Add a handful of clean roots to a quart of water and boil for up to an hour, or until the liquid turns a dark red. In the South, it's a popular beverage hot or iced; I love it over ice, barely sweetened. For years, sassafras was the primary

These fresh green leaves will make excellent filé powder, once they've been dried and crushed.

flavoring in root beer, but it was replaced when the FDA decided that safrole — the essential oil in sassafras — might cause cancer. (The leaves don't contain enough safrole to be considered dangerous, however.) To put things in perspective, the toxicity of sassafras is roughly half that of alcohol. While I would never dream of telling you what to do, I continue to drink sassafras tea.

Sassafras twig syrup makes another delicious drink. To make it, gather six to eight twigs, each about 6 inches long. Peel away some of the bark (to release flavor), and boil the twigs for 10 minutes in a quart of water. Allow the decoction to steep for 8 hours or overnight, then strain twigs out and measure your liquid. Combine with sugar and bring to a boil to make a simple syrup. If you like a heavy syrup, use equal parts sugar and decoction. I adjust my sugar depending on the ultimate use. For ice cream, try 2 parts sugar to 1 part decoction. To make a cocktail or soft drink, use 1 part sugar, then combine this mixer with alcohol or seltzer.

Young sassafras leaves, ready to harvest.

## IS SAFROLE SAFE?

In 1976 the FDA banned safrole as a potential carcinogen. However, this decision is controversial among foragers. No studies have been done on human reactions to safrole, and the amount needed to produce a toxic endpoint in mice (where 50 percent of the animals died) is approximately 10 times higher than the dose estimated to be harmful to humans if consumed on a regular basis.

I choose to enjoy sassafras teas for several reasons: 1) No case of safrole toxicity in humans has ever been recorded. 2) The FDA studies were performed with concentrated, lab-produced safrole oil, which is much stronger than the safrole released from sassafras bark by boiling. 3) Safrole occurs in small amounts in other spices such as cinnamon and black pepper, so we're not exactly living in a safrole-free world. 4) The cynic in me suspects that the government's ban may have something to do with the fact that safrole oil is an ingredient in ecstasy. I leave it to each of you, my intelligent, discerning readers, to decide what's best for yourself.

# CHAPTER 8

# FRIENDLY FUNGI:
# Five Easy Mushrooms

I harvested these premium fungi from my Pennsylvania yard.
One of the many benefits of not cultivating a lawn!

# Mushrooms are about as exciting as foraging gets,

so it's no wonder they call it mushroom hunting. (Have you ever heard the phrase "the thrill of the gather"?) Grown women have been known to leap and squeal when they find a good harvest . . . or so I've heard.

## Mushrooms 101

What is it that makes mushrooms so intriguing and irresistible? Maybe because they aren't as reliably perennial as plants. The underground mycelium (a mushroom's equivalent to a root system) can lie dormant during years of adverse conditions, not producing any fungal growth aboveground. You might remember exactly where you harvested plentiful chanterelles one year, only to have a dry season in which not a single mushroom appears. Or maybe it's because fungi are so ephemeral. A few days can make the difference between delicious, tender mushrooms and inedible mush.

Mushroom flavors are complex and unique, dark and subtle; they add an unmistakable earthiness to any dish. And while some are large and showy enough to practically jump out at you from the landscape, others hide in leaf litter and moss, forcing you to get down on your hands and knees. But you'll be glad you did. No bland cultivated button mushroom can deliver the satisfaction of a flavorful wild mushroom.

Nevertheless, mushrooms may still seem scary to some. The best route is to start by foraging one of the several species that have no poisonous look-alikes and that may even grow in your own yard. All of the species mentioned in this chapter are good for beginners. And for extra safety, keep in mind these caveats:

**Cook all mushrooms.** I know you see raw button mushrooms sliced into salads, but it's not a great idea. Raw mushrooms are tough for humans to digest, because their cell walls are composed of chitin, not cellulose. Cooking can make them more nutritious by breaking down cell walls and releasing nutrients. Also, some mushrooms that would actually cause stomach upset can be rendered harmless and desirable by cooking. Finally, cooking kills any evil hitchhikers like insects or bacteria.

**Wash all mushrooms.** Despite what you've heard, it's perfectly all right to wash your mushrooms; you can even *soak* them to get them clean. Rumors circulate that washing will turn your mushrooms mushy or dilute their taste. This simply isn't true. It's much easier to clean your mushrooms with water than by dry brushing and rubbing, so go ahead. They absorb very little water in the process, and what they do absorb will be very quickly released in either cooking or dehydrating, making the entire discussion irrelevant. If you don't believe me ask Alton Brown, Harold Magee, or Jacques Pepin.

**NEVER eat a mushroom you're not 100 percent certain of.** I know I've said that about foraging in general, but the stakes are especially high with mushrooms. In general, the non-gilled mushrooms are safer to start with. (See Gills or No Gills? on page 193.)

If mushrooms thrill you as much as they thrill me, buy yourself 5 or 10 excellent field guides. Take some classes and some walking tours. Learn to make spore prints. Knowledge is power. It will keep you alive.

# GILLS OR NO GILLS?

The best way to avoid harvesting a poisonous mushroom is simply to avoid any mushroom that has gills. The undersides of fungi can generally be described in three ways: gilled, pored, or toothed. Gills are thin flaps of tissue that run parallel to each other. Gilled mushrooms are the most common type of mushroom; an edible example you might be familiar with is the oyster mushroom. Pores are small holes in a spongy surface; the porcini is an example of a pored mushroom. The caps of toothed mushrooms are covered with little pointed teeth. These are less common than either gilled or pored mushrooms. Hedgehog (a.k.a. sweet tooth) mushrooms are toothed mushrooms.

The underside of a mushroom provides valuable information! Above from left: pores, gills, and teeth. For the beginning forager, pored and toothed mushrooms are safer choices.

# BLACK TRUMPET

*Craterellus fallax* and *C. cornucopioides*

**What it is:** a mushroom, related to chanterelles
**Where to find it:** in mixed woods, often in moss
**Edible parts:** the trumpet

## THE DETAILS

Black trumpets are sneaky little mushrooms. They most often grow near oak and beech trees, in conjunction with moss. Since they're low-lying and the color of soil, it's not easy to spot them until you're right on top of them. The first time I found black trumpets in our lawn (and that's using the term loosely), I went inside to confirm my identification in several field guides. When I came back outside, I couldn't find the mushrooms again, even though I knew where to look.

The black trumpet is a safe mushroom for beginners, because it has no poisonous look-alikes. They're also crazy delicious, and just a few will impart a strong and wonderful taste to your cooking. This is a midsummer to early fall mushroom and grows best in part to full shade, after some soaking rain. If you're a lawn aficionado who regularly tends your grass with herbicides and frequent mowings, you probably won't find black trumpets (or any other mushroom) in your front yard, but my definition of a lawn is more liberal than most. If it's soft and green, I'm happy. No herbicides and no fertilizers makes for a large patch of moss and weeds sprinkled with some very tasty fungi. Works for me.

## HOW TO HARVEST

Black trumpets are small mushrooms. They grow to a maximum of 2 to 3 inches tall, but under many growing conditions they may not get larger than an inch. Which means you have a decision to make: Should you harvest them as soon as you find them, or wait until they reach their maximum size? My judgment is usually clouded by greed, so I do a little of both. I harvest the largest mushrooms when I first see them, just in case something happens to prevent my harvesting later (dry weather makes them shrivel, slugs eat them, the world ends), and I leave the smallest ones to check on in a few days. I'm sure you'll find your own compromise.

Because black trumpets usually grow in moss, they are among the cleaner mushrooms to harvest. Gently grip the bottom of the trumpet and pull; it will come right off in your hand, perhaps with a little bit of moss attached, but without the clods of dirt that often accompany mushroom gathering. Also, since these are not gilled mushrooms, they're easy to clean with a quick rinse. If you don't have time to use them right away, they dry well and can be rehydrated with little, if any, loss of flavor.

## HOW TO EAT IT

Leave smaller trumpets whole, and cut larger mushrooms in half or quarters. A simple sauté in butter, a little garlic, and a dash of salt showcases the taste of the black trumpet. You can use it in rice, over pasta, on bruschetta, or in eggs. Or make a sauce with white wine and butter and use the mushrooms over chicken or fish. Black trumpets are fragrant and have a taste that never disappoints.

> The black trumpet is a safe mushroom for beginners, because it has no poisonous look-alikes. They're also crazy delicious.

If you find yourself walking through dappled late-summer sun in mossy woods, stop and look down at your feet. You might be walking on black trumpet mushrooms!

SPRING SUMMER FALL WINTER

# CHICKEN-OF-THE-WOODS, SULPHUR SHELF

## *Laetiporus sulphureus* and *L. cincinnatus*

**What it is:** a polypore mushroom
**Where to find it:** on trees, logs, roots
**Edible parts:** mushroom brackets

> I don't think the chicken mushroom tastes like chicken. But its texture makes it a useful chicken substitute in casseroles, soups, stews, and pastas.

### THE DETAILS

Chicken-of-the-woods is not the same as hen-of-the-woods. It's unfortunate the names are so similar, because the mushrooms themselves are very different. Hens were so named because someone thought they looked like the ruffled tails of poultry. Chickens were so named because someone thought they (wait for it . . . ) tasted like chicken! They sure don't look like chicken. These mushrooms are easily visible from a car window at 50 miles per hour. The tops are bright orange and the undersides are either yellow or white, depending on the species. Both are polypores with no poisonous look-alikes.

Like hens, chickens are large mushrooms that regrow in the same spot year after year until they kill their host tree, then continue a few years after that until all the wood's nutrients are exhausted. Unlike hens, chickens don't always grow at the base of trees; you'll often find them higher up on the trunk. They grow in the shade of mixed woods and the full sun of city parks.

The two chicken mushroom species recommended here, *L. sulphureus* and *L. cincinnatus*, grow on hardwood trees and are safe to eat when properly prepared and if you don't have a specific allergy. However, several closely related species (*L. gilbertsonii* and *L. conifericola* on the West Coast and *L. hueroniensis* in the Midwest) may be more problematic. These three species grow on eucalyptus and conifer trees and are more likely to cause gastric upset than the hardwood chickens. Many people eat them without any trouble, but to be on the safe side, if you can't identify the host tree, just keep on walking.

### HOW TO HARVEST

Chicken-of-the-woods gets tough as it ages (although *L. cincinnatus* is generally considered to be more tender than *L. sulphureus*), so break off a piece before you harvest. If the central core of the mushroom feels woody, you may still be able to trim tender, newer growth from the outer edges of the brackets. Use

The unmistakable bright orange color of the chicken mushroom makes it an easy mushroom for beginners to harvest safely.

a knife to cut the brackets off the bark, and look in between them for insects. Chickens that are past their prime may harbor flies and wormy intruders, and some people actually get sick from eating older specimens. So stick with the young and tender bits.

If you're really lucky, you'll find a young chicken (dare I call it a chick?), emerging from a tree trunk or log with just a blush of orange on its young yellow flesh. Don't hesitate! It may be smaller than a mature specimen, but the tender texture and delicate taste are superb.

## HOW TO EAT IT

I don't think the chicken mushroom tastes like chicken. But its texture makes it a useful chicken substitute in casseroles, soups, stews, and pastas. It's a large, meaty mushroom that stands up to baking and braising. If you find a chicken slightly past its prime but still bug-free, it's worth taking home for stock or duxelles (see page 199). It's not unusual to find a large chicken, so if you bring home more than you can use before the mushroom goes bad, sauté and freeze your extra. This mushroom also stores well dried, but it should be cooked with extra fat after rehydration.

SPRING    SUMMER    FALL    WINTER

# HEDGEHOG, SWEET TOOTH

## *Hydnum repandum* and *H. umbilicatum*

**What it is:** a toothed mushroom

**Where to find it:** on the ground, among hardwoods and conifers

**Edible parts:** mushroom cap

The tiny teeth of hedgehog mushrooms hang down like mini-stalactites.

## THE DETAILS

These tasty mushrooms have no poisonous look-alikes and are easy to identify. They grow singly, often scattered in large groups. Their caps have an irregular shape and are orangey, with lighter-colored stalks. *Hydnum repandum* may grow to be 6 inches in diameter, while *H. umbilicatum* is smaller, with a darker cap. Both are equally tasty.

Some people confuse hedgehogs with chanterelles, but a quick look at the underside of the orange cap will clarify matters. These mushrooms are neither gilled nor pored. They have short, spiny teeth that hang down like mini-stalactites, and the underside of the cap is beige, while chanterelles are orange top and bottom.

## HOW TO HARVEST

Hedgehog mushrooms fruit from summer through mid fall. They may grow to be several inches across. Since they're seldom bothered by insects, you can leave them to grow without worrying that slugs or beetles will beat you to the harvest. These mushrooms are tricky to clean because of their numerous, delicate teeth; you're better off keeping them clean from the start. To do so, slice the stalk of the mushroom just above the ground, leaving dirt and conifer needles behind rather than

> Hedgehogs have a firm texture that stands up to various methods of preparation. They have a nutty, delicate flavor that is best appreciated on its own.

including them with your harvest.

Older (larger) specimens may be slightly bitter, but a quick blanch before cooking will remove the bitter taste. To test, put a small piece in your mouth, chew, and spit it out. If it tastes bitter, blanch and then cook.

## HOW TO EAT IT

Even small specimens have a firm texture that stands up to various methods of preparation. They have a nutty, delicate flavor that is best appreciated on its own or combined with mild flavors like eggs or rice. Because this mushroom absorbs a surprising amount of liquid, it takes on the taste of whatever cooking liquid you use. I suggest a simple side dish of sautéed sweet tooths (say it five times fast).

### DUXELLES

Duxelles is a wonderful item to keep on hand in your kitchen. It's a mixture of minced mushrooms, onions, and herbs, sautéed in butter and reduced to a paste. (You might even add a splash of wine!) Duxelles is a classic French preparation, traditionally used in beef Wellington and veal Orloff, but it has many more uses in today's kitchen. It can be stored frozen, then thawed to flavor sauces, soups, or eggs, or to serve on top of crostini or pizza.

SPRING  SUMMER  FALL  WINTER

# HEN-OF-THE-WOODS, MAITAKE

*Grifola frondosa*

**What it is:** a polypore mushroom
**Where to find it:** at the base of hardwood trees, often oaks
**Edible parts:** mushroom caps

## THE DETAILS

Like many mushrooms, hen-of-the-woods can be hard to spot in its native habitat. It's often found at the base of oak trees. Since its color is somewhere between that of oak bark and that of fallen oak leaves, well, let's just say it doesn't jump out and scream, "Pick me, pick me!" When you do spot one, however, you're likely to make a major haul. It's not unusual for a large hen to weigh many pounds.

Whether you call it hen-of-the-woods or maitake (two names, one mushroom), this meaty bracket fungus has excellent taste and substance. It grows on wood in shade to part shade. If the fungus clump appears at a small distance from the base of the tree, you can bet it's actually growing from the buried roots. You're likely to find it growing in the same place, year after year, until (sadly) it kills the host tree. Circle of life.

Hen-of-the-woods is a fast-growing, early-fall mushroom that appears after soaking rain. The undersides of the mushroom have pores, not gills, making it a polypore. Superficially (but not really) it resembles one other mushroom, the black-staining polypore (*Meripilus sumstinei*). Fortunately this is also edible, although not as delicious as maitake, so if you make a mistake you're in no danger. But you won't make a mistake, because you would never eat something you weren't 100 percent sure of, *would you?* Besides, once you've picked the black-staining polypore you'll know it! They don't call it "black-staining" for nothing. It takes days to get your fingers clean.

## HOW TO HARVEST

It helps to carry a knife with you when hunting for mushrooms, especially mushrooms that grow on wood. A sharp blade allows you to slice off the fungus without damaging the tree's bark. Young hens are tender and clean. Older specimens may be tough and buggy, so break off a few pieces before harvesting a giant clump. If it smells fresh (in a fungal way) and looks free of insects, carve yourself a hunk and bring it home.

The thrill of mushroom hunting often leads to impulsiveness and irrationality. Or so I hear. If you find hens in your own yard, by all means, take

Hen-of-the-woods mushrooms are often giant, providing good eats for many meals to come.

them all. If you're foraging in a park and there's more mushroom than you need (I trust you to define "need" for yourself), leave a clump behind for the next eager forager to come along. It's good mushroom karma.

Maitake is one of the few mushrooms that can be frozen without blanching or cooking. Clean it, cut it into cooking-size pieces, then freeze. It can also be frozen after a quick sauté, or dried and reconstituted later.

## HOW TO EAT IT

The caps of hen-of-the-woods are the tender, choice part of the mushroom. We'll get to those in a minute. Numerous caps branch off a tough, fibrous white stem. But don't throw the stem away! The cleaned stalk can be used to make mushroom stock, or minced and made into duxelles. (See Duxelles, page 199.)

As for those choice caps, let yourself have some fun. Hen-of-the-woods is substantial enough to be served as a main course. I hesitate to say "meat substitute" because it

tastes nothing like meat. But it can add meatlike substance to pasta dishes, casseroles, and stir-fries. At least once in your life, try roasted hen-of-the-woods. To make it, break off bite-size pieces, toss them in melted butter or olive oil, salt, and pepper, then spread them on a cookie sheet and bake at 400°F for 15 minutes. Check and turn or stir to cook evenly, then return them to the oven, checking every 5 minutes until the edges just start to turn crispy. I can't begin to describe how delicious these are.

SPRING SUMMER FALL WINTER

# OYSTER MUSHROOM

## *Pleurotus ostreatus*

**What it is:** a gilled mushroom
**Where to find it:** on trees, stumps, logs
**Edible parts:** mushroom cap

Oyster mushrooms have a mild taste and tender texture.

## THE DETAILS

This mushroom grows in clumps on dead and dying wood. Oyster mushrooms usually colonize hard-woods such as oak, beech, and alder, but they may occasionally grow on coni-fers. Oyster mushrooms grow year-round but are most plentiful in fall. They tolerate colder tempera-tures than many other mushrooms, which means that even after a frost or two (with adequate rain) you can count on oyster mushrooms for your winter table. I've harvested frozen oysters from tree stumps, then brought them home to thaw into perfect, delectable speci-mens. Because oysters can be grown commercially, you can familiarize your-self with how they look in your local supermarket. General characteristics

> Oyster mushrooms are most plentiful in fall. They tolerate colder temperatures than many other mushrooms, which means that even after a frost or two you can count on oyster mushrooms for your winter table.

to look out for: smooth, brown to off-white caps, white gills, and a small off-center or lateral stem.

## HOW TO HARVEST

Ask yourself the age-old mushroom harvesting question: Would I rather have a few small, perfect mushrooms now or risk them for the chance of more, larger mushrooms next week? Once you've figured that out, use a knife to slice between the mushroom's base and the bark of the tree. Check in between the gills of larger caps for bugs, then clean your mushrooms and either cook or store. Oysters dry well and can also be sautéed, then frozen.

You may find oyster mushrooms growing from dead tree stumps or logs.

## HOW TO EAT IT

Large, meaty oyster caps can be grilled, broiled, or fried like steaks with butter and garlic. They can also be used in all the traditional mushroom ways: soups, pastas, risottos. You'll probably only eat the tender caps, reserving the tougher stems for stock. For an unusual seasonal dish, ask yourself what else is found in abundance in autumn. If you said acorns, you're reading my mind. Acorn mushroom soup is thick and hearty and tastes like the embodiment of fall.

# Grow Your Own Mushrooms

Not all mushrooms can be cultivated, but many can. If you're planting an edible garden, why not include some fungi?

Many mushrooms that grow on wood eventually kill their host trees, so I'm not suggesting you cultivate a crop of fungi on the regal oak that shades your home and gives you acorns. The easiest way to grow mushrooms is to buy a kit, which consists of a growing substrate (often straw or sawdust) that has been inoculated with mushroom spawn. Spawn is another word for young mycelium, the underground portion (corresponding to plants' roots) of a fungus. There

Shiitake mushrooms are easy to grow by inoculating fresh logs with plug spawn.

are several reliable vendors of this type of kit that offer several different mushroom varieties, including oyster, shiitake, wine caps, and shaggy manes. (See page 227.)

Growing mushrooms as part of your outdoor garden is a little trickier than growing an indoor kit, but it may be even more rewarding. You can produce a larger crop that will come back for several years. (Indoor kits usually produce one or two flushes of fungi and run their course within 6 to 8 weeks.) Some mushrooms grow best on logs, while others thrive in a prepared substrate, much like a garden bed. For these, you'll prepare a growing area with straw, hardwood mulch, compost, or a combination of these materials, depending on the mushroom. You'll inoculate the growing material with spawn, then water and wait. Don't worry, you don't have to remember all this. Instructions come with each kit, explaining how to prepare the growing area, when to inoculate, and how often to water. Many mushrooms can be grown side by side with plants, which is especially nice if you don't have enough space for a dedicated mushroom patch.

If you'd rather grow mushrooms on hardwood, you don't have to sacrifice your beloved trees. You will need to do a little research to learn which kind of wood your mushroom crop prefers, and you'll need a source for logs of that type of wood. Oak is generally a good wood for mushroom growing; softwoods like pine are generally not. You'll need freshly cut logs, to minimize the chances that the wood has already been colonized by a competing fungus.

The easiest way to inoculate a log is to order spawn in plug or dowel form. Use an electric drill to drill holes in the log, then place one plug in each hole and cover the plug with melted beeswax. The logs should be kept in shade and watered regularly, and they may take as long as a year or two to produce mushrooms. (Again, don't worry about memorizing these directions. Spawn packages come with instructions.) If you like the idea of a mushroom log but don't want to go in search of fresh-cut lumber, you can order a log already inoculated with shiitake spawn from Lost Creek Mushroom Farm (see page 227).

For foragers with patience who like to experiment, planting a mushroom log is a great project. Logs often produce for 4 to 5 years, until the nutrients in the wood are used up.

# CHAPTER 9

# YOU WOULDN'T DO THIS IF IT DIDN'T TASTE GOOD:

# Preserving Advice and Basic Recipes

A cool, light spruce-tip sorbet makes an unusual dessert or palate cleanser.

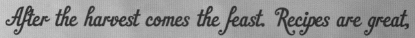

*After the harvest comes the feast.* Recipes are great, but equally important is learning general techniques for how to make the most of your harvest. It won't be long before you're making up your own recipes.

I'll touch on several food preservation techniques in this chapter, but this isn't really a food preservation book. For more information on various methods and equipment, please see Resources and Recommended Reading (page 225).

# Freezing

Freezing is a familiar technique, and you might not think you need instructions on how to freeze. But a few tips will make your frozen harvest taste better and brighter when you cook with it.

## Leaves and Stems

Most leaves and stems should be blanched before freezing, for several reasons:

- Blanching stops the activity of enzymes that break down plant tissue and cause degradation of flavor and texture.

- Blanching cleans the harvest and brightens the color.

- Blanching wilts leaves and shoots, making them easier to pack and store.

After blanching, cool your cooked vegetables quickly and thoroughly to stop the cooking process. Have a pot of ice water nearby and submerge your blanched vegetables, then allow them to drain completely before freezing. Ice crystals may form if food is frozen while it's still wet, and that doesn't taste good.

## Mushrooms, Fruit, and Nuts

Many mushrooms freeze better if they're cooked before freezing. They can be sautéed in butter or oil, then frozen along with their cooking liquid.

Fruits and berries freeze better when they're frozen individually rather than packaged together. If you've had an especially impressive Juneberry or mulberry harvest, spread it out on a cookie sheet covered in wax paper, then put the cookie sheet in the freezer. When the individual berries have frozen, you can slide them off the cookie sheet into a container to package and store them together. This way, berries maintain their structure and will be free of ice crystals.

Nuts can be frozen shelled or unshelled. If you're not planning to work with them within a week of harvesting, freezing is a good idea. Nuts are generally high in fat, which means they spoil quickly if left out on the counter. Some nuts require curing or drying before they're shelled, and can then be stored in the freezer for up to a year.

# Dehydration

Drying is a great way to preserve the pure taste of an ingredient. Fruits and mushrooms dried at low temperatures can be stored for years, then rehydrated to use them just as you'd use fresh. If you don't have a dehydrator, spread your bounty on a cookie sheet and dry it in the oven at 125°F. If you can't get your oven that low, set it to the lowest temperature possible and leave the door open a crack. Dehydration is essential for making fruit leather and fruit paste.

Hedgehog mushrooms, ready for the dehydrator.

## Fruit Leather

Fruit leather makes a healthy snack and can also be rehydrated and used to make sauces or marinades. The fruit must be cooked before dehydrating. Small fruits (Juneberries,

Fruit leather is a great way to make use of an odd assortment of foraged fruits.

silverberries, mulberries) can be cooked whole, while larger fruits (crab apples, pineapple guava, prickly pear) should be cut into smaller pieces. Spread a layer of fruit on the bottom of a large pan and cover with water. Cook over medium heat until the fruit is soft enough to mash, then purée in a blender or run through a food mill if the pulp is especially seedy.

Taste the fruit, and decide whether it needs sweetening. Some tart fruits, like crab apples and silverberries, cry out for sugar, honey, or agave nectar. Return the pulp to the pan and sweeten, if necessary. Start with ½ tablespoon per cup of pulp and increase the sweetener until you're happy with the taste of the fruit. Cook over medium heat until the consistency is thick enough to be spreadable, but not runny.

If you have a dehydrator, spread a layer of pulp on your trays (lined with fruit leather sheets), about ⅛-inch thick. It will take approximately 8 to 12 hours to dry. If you don't have a dehydrator, place a sheet of parchment paper on a cookie sheet and pour the fruit pulp in a ⅛-inch layer. Dry this in the oven at 125 to 150°F overnight, or until the leather is dry and flexible.

Once you have achieved leather, peel it off the trays or parchment and cut it into small pieces or strips. Store in an airtight container in the refrigerator.

Don't be afraid to combine fruits. Just as sour fruits may need sweetener, other berries benefit from a little tartness. The sweet, soft fruits of the strawberry tree taste better and brighter with a little acidity; try flowering quince, crab apples, or mountain ash berries. Pomegranates add both flavor and color.

Strawberry tree/pomegranate fruit paste will soon be a tart and tasty fruit leather.

## Membrillo

Membrillo (a.k.a. quince paste) is a classic Spanish dessert. Most recipes call for traditional quinces (*Cydonia oblonga*), sugar, and water . . . that's it. My version uses ornamental quinces (*Chaenomeles* species), vanilla, and a Meyer lemon. It's time-consuming, I admit. But it's delicious, and guaranteed to impress.

Quarter your ornamental quinces (no need to peel or core), and place them in a shallow pan with just enough water to cover the fruit. For every 4 pounds of fruit, add 1 vanilla bean and the juice and rind of a lemon. Cook over medium heat until the fruit is fork-tender. Remove the vanilla bean, and scrape its seeds into the pan. Remove the lemon peel and run the cooked fruit through a food mill. This removes the quince peel and copious seeds.

Measure the fruit pulp and return it to your pan, adding an equal amount of sugar. Set over medium heat and simmer, stirring occasionally, for 2 hours, plus or minus. The pulp will turn a deep red color. When most of the water has evaporated, the pulp will be quite thick but still stirrable. Transfer it to a shallow dish, cake pan, or cookie sheet lined with buttered parchment paper. The membrillo should be about an inch thick.

You still need to dry your quince paste, either in the oven (lowest possible temperature, with door open) or in the dehydrator. If your cake pan or cookie sheet fits in your dehydrator, slide it in and set the temperature to 135°F. (Mine doesn't, so I use the oven.) Check it every 2 hours for dryness; you'll want to feel a little give when you poke it with your finger, but it shouldn't maintain a dent. Drying could take

Membrillo pairs well with sharp cheeses like manchego.

8 to 12 hours. Remove the membrillo from the pan, then wrap it up and refrigerate. It keeps for months. The end product should be dense, slightly sticky, and easy to slice. The taste is complex: rich, tart, and sweet. Serve it with slices of manchego or sharp cheddar cheese for an ambrosial, sophisticated snack.

# Syrups, Jams, and Jellies

Creating a high-sugar, low-water environment is another way to preserve food. Sugar makes food inhospitable to microbes. It binds to water molecules and draws moisture out of living cells, thus killing them. This is why jams, jellies, and syrups, when properly cooked and sealed, can be safely stored without refrigeration. Once open, they last in the refrigerator for a very long time.

Syrups can be used in many ways. They can be poured on top of cake or ice cream, frozen to make sorbets or popsicles, or used as unusual cocktail ingredients. Fruit syrups are made in much the same way as jams or jellies (see below), but they are cooked for less time and to a thinner consistency. Flowers and herbs are first brewed in a simple syrup, then strained.

## Milkweed Flower Syrup

Milkweed flowers make a syrup that is both delicious and lovely to look at. The blooms imbue the syrup with their pink-purple color and a taste that is not only sweetly floral but also vaguely tart. It looks lovely in white wine or bubbly; think of it as a wildflower version of Kir Royale. For dessert, pour the syrup into popsicle molds and freeze overnight, or use an ice cream maker to create a delicate sorbet.

To make the syrup, place 2 cups of fully opened, dripping-with-nectar milkweed flowers in a pot with 4 cups of water and 2 cups of sugar. Stir gently with a wire whisk to dissolve the sugar, then bring to a boil. Turn down the heat and simmer until the volume is reduced by half and the taste pleases you. Better to start with a lighter syrup and add sugar if you want more sweetness.

Milkweed flower syrup can be turned into a delicious sorbet.

## Mountain Ash Jelly

Most of the jelly recipes you find online these days call for additional pectin. In many instances this is necessary; if you're making jelly with a low-pectin fruit, by all means, choose a commercial pectin and follow the directions on the box. The pectin-sugar-acid relationship is a specific one, so when I say follow the directions, I mean *precisely*. Be aware that some of the low-sugar pectins produce a tasty but not crystal-clear jelly.

That being said, it bugs me when recipes require commercial pectin for a fruit that already has plenty of pectin on its own. I think recipe writers include it because commercial pectin pretty much guarantees success, and they don't want their readers to be disappointed. But I want you to experience the joy that comes from achieving a perfect jell *without* the addition of commercial pectin. Trust me, it's a thrill.

Of the fruits covered in this book, ornamental quinces, crab apples, cornelian cherries, Oregon grapes, and mountain ash (rowan) berries are the best candidates for a no-pectin-added jelly. All have lots of natural pectin and very quickly and obviously reach the jelling point. The color of mountain ash jelly is a gorgeous, clear vermilion.

Mountain ash jelly is traditionally used as a condiment with meats like lamb, venison, and pork.

Place mountain ash berries in a shallow pan and barely cover them with water. Bring to a boil, then reduce heat and simmer until the berries are soft. Mash with a potato masher, then pour through a wet jelly bag. (Moistening the jelly bag prevents it from absorbing your valuable juice.) Leave the juice to drip for several hours or overnight. Don't squeeze the bag to hurry the process, or the jelly will be cloudy and you won't win first prize at the county fair. If you absolutely can't wait, you can twist the jelly bag from the top, which speeds the dripping process. Resist the temptation to squeeze directly.

Measure your juice and return it to your jelly pan. For every cup of juice, add ¾ cup sugar and 1 tablespoon lemon juice. Don't process more than 4 cups of juice at a time, or your jelly may not jell. (If you want to know why, see Pectin Bonds, page 215.)

Bring the mixture to a boil, stirring regularly. When the bubbles become small and uniform, start testing for the jelling point. To do this, scoop a spoonful of liquid with a large metal

A few crab apples augment the mountain ash berries. Mash and stir the fruit, then allow the pulp to drip through a jelly bag, collecting the juice.

When two drops on the edge of a spoon slide into one, you've reached the jelling point.

spoon and hold it over your jelly pan, allowing the liquid to drip back down into the pan. As cooking progresses, the drops become thicker and the last bit of each spoonful falls from the bowl of the spoon in two or three thick drops. The jelling point is reached when these final drops slide together at the edge of the spoon to form a single, large drop that slides off the spoon in a single sheeting motion. There are several other ways to test for the jelling point (a candy thermometer, the wrinkle test), but the spoon test is most conclusive and reliable.

When the jelling point is reached, remove your jelly from the heat immediately, and pour into sterilized jars. Cap the jars and seal in a boiling water bath for 10 minutes, then remove and listen for the popping lids that indicate you have successfully vacuum-sealed your

jars. Different jellies take different amounts of time to set, but mountain ash jelly sets quickly, in a matter of hours. Some jellies take several weeks.

## Juneberry Jam

Juneberries don't have much natural pectin, so you'll need to add pectin to make a jelly, either by combining Juneberries with a high-pectin fruit like crab apples or adding commercial pectin. However, because Juneberries don't have large seeds, they also lend themselves to jam, which uses the entire fruit rather than just the strained juice. Firmly set jams can be made with commercial pectin, but you can make a soft jam without additional pectin if you have the patience to cook the fruit down slowly. I'm not usually a patient person, but when it comes to food, I'm willing to sacrifice speed and convenience for great taste. Since commercial pectin recipes require considerably more sugar than recipes made without commercial pectin, the taste of the fruit can be overwhelmed by generic sweetness. The unique taste of the Juneberry deserves better than that. For a soft-set jam that shows off the complex taste of the berry (without clobbering it with sweetness), try this recipe without added pectin.

## PECTIN BONDS

Pectin is released from fruit cell walls via the application of heat, but too much heat can break down the network of pectin fibers that allows jelly to jell. If you work with more than 4 cups of juice, the length of time it takes to reach the jelling point may result in irreparably broken pectin bonds.

Measure your Juneberries and place them in your jelly pan. Barely cover the berries with water, and bring the mixture to a boil, then reduce to a simmer. As the fruit softens, mash with a potato masher. For every cup of fruit, add ¾ cup of sugar and whisk it into the fruit. Taste your mixture and evaluate. If you like the taste, increase the heat to medium, to create a regular but not rolling boil. If you'd like a little acidity, add 1 tablespoon of citrus juice for each cup of fruit. Personally, I think the sweetness of Juneberries is nicely highlighted by the tartness of lemon, lime, orange, or grapefruit juice.

Continue to stir your fruit mixture with a large metal spoon, testing for thickness every few minutes. Remember that the jam will continue to thicken as it cools. When you're satisfied with the consistency, remove from the heat, pour into jars, and process as you would any jam: 10 minutes in a boiling water bath.

# Booze

Alcohol is an excellent preservative. And it's fun to drink. For those of you with patience, consider making wine. You can make a small batch without much specialized equipment, using any number of plants. My favorite homemade wines include silverberry, Juneberry, Japanese knotweed, lilac, and dandelion. But be aware, winemaking is a commitment. Most recipes need one to two years to mature and become delicious. Liqueurs deliver more immediate gratification.

A gallon of crabapple wine with an airlock is surrounded by several other wild vintages.

## Purple Fruits Liqueur

Gather together your stray fruits and berries and cut them into bite-size pieces, if necessary. I use whatever I have on hand: quinces, sumac berries, or strawberry tree fruit. You can make a liqueur with any combination you like or use one fruit for a singular taste.

If you find yourself with small amounts of several different fruits (not enough for jam or ice cream), why not combine them to make a jewel-colored fruity liqueur, which you can sip plain or mix into a creative cocktail?

Measure your fruit and set aside. For this batch, I used a combination of purple fruits (American beautyberry, Oregon grape, elderberry, Juneberry, and mulberry) that I knew would make a vibrant-colored liqueur. Measure out an equal volume of sugar — for example, for every cup of berries, measure out a cup of sugar. Find a large glass jar that accommodates twice the combined volume of sugar and fruit. Pour a layer of fruit into the jar, then sprinkle with a layer of sugar. Alternate layers of fruit and sugar until everything is used up, then fill the jar with vodka or your liquor of choice. I like the neutrality of vodka for most fruits, but sometimes the taste of gin or rum is just what

Mixing layers of fruit with layers of sugar is the first step in making liqueur.

the bartender ordered. Swirl it around and keep it out of direct sun for the next few weeks, swirling to mix whenever you remember (two or three times a day).

After two or three weeks, strain off the fruit and bottle the booze. Since I can't bear to waste food, I use the vodka-soaked fruit to make drunken jelly. If you don't have a sweet tooth, you can still create your own liqueurs. Spice some vodka with wild ginger, spicebush berries, sweetfern leaves, or juniper berries.

Vodka takes on the color and taste of the purple berries. Mix it with seltzer for a unique, carbonated cocktail.

## Dandelion Wine

Some oenophiles look down their noses at wines made from anything other than grapes. They don't know what they're missing. Most fruits, many vegetables, and a surprising number of flowers and herbs can be used to make delicious wines. If winemaking becomes a serious hobby, you'll want to invest in some specialized equipment and a few ingredients, but for a first attempt you can make do with stuff you have around the house.

This recipe is for a gallon of dandelion wine. With a few adjustments, it will work for lilac or linden flowers, Japanese knotweed shoots, or any number of fruits.

First, collect 6 cups of dandelion petals, removed from the green calyces that hold the petals together at the base of each flower. This is the tedious part. You'll need about 3 quarts of whole flowers to get enough petals, and it will take patience to hold and twist the petals out of each individual bloom. If you get impatient, you can do a little at a time and freeze the petals until you have enough for a batch of wine.

Deposit the petals in a large, nonreactive pot and add the juice of 1 large lemon, the juice of 1 medium orange, a teaspoon of grated ginger root (wild or from the grocery store), 2½ pounds of sugar, and 1 gallon of water. Bring the mixture to a boil, then reduce heat and simmer for 30 minutes. Strain the liquid into a sterile, food-grade plastic bucket and let it cool until it reaches body temperature. (When you touch the outside of the bucket, it should feel neither warm nor cold.)

If you don't have an airlock for your jug, a glove or balloon with a single pinprick will do the trick.

Next, add a package of wine yeast; I like champagne yeast for dandelion wine. Cover and let it sit for a week, stirring daily, if possible. (The world won't end if you go away for the weekend and can't stir it every day.) After a week, pour the cloudy wine into a 1-gallon glass jug or large jar, leaving behind the layer of yeast and sediment (a.k.a. "lees") that has settled on the bottom. Fit a balloon over the top of the bottle, or use an elastic band to attach a latex glove over the opening. Use a pin to poke a single hole in the balloon or glove to allow gasses to escape during fermentation.

Store in a cool, dark place and check again in three months. If ¼ inch of lees has accumulated, it's time to rack again. When the wine has cleared, bottle it and store in the dark. Dandelion wine gets better with age. The longer you wait, the greater will be your reward. Two years will make you very happy.

Dandelion wine is the color of sunshine.

# Baked Goods and Savory Dishes

Simple dishes like quiches, omelettes, and pies are excellent vehicles for edible greens, and you probably already have favorite recipes you can use. Just substitute hosta shoots or milkweed florets for asparagus or broccoli flowers. But when it comes to baked goods, an actual recipe comes in handy. These two quick-bread recipes make excellent use of foraged ingredients. The dahlia tuber bread is sweet and spicy, while the acorn bread is savory and rich.

## Dahlia Tuber Bread

Dahlia tubers contribute moisture and carbohydrates to this dense quick bread. If you have a favorite zucchini bread recipe, simply substitute grated dahlia tubers for grated zucchini. Or try this one.

In a small bowl, whisk together two eggs, 1½ teaspoons vanilla, and ½ cup vegetable oil. In a second bowl, combine 1 cup sugar, 1½ cups flour, and ½ teaspoon each baking powder, baking soda, and salt. While traditional recipes suggest cinnamon and nutmeg as spices, I

Dahlia tubers (cleaned, peeled, and shredded) make an interesting quick bread.

prefer 2 teaspoons of ground spicebush berries and 2 teaspoons of ground wild ginger. Add these to your dry ingredients and mix well.

Next, fold the liquid ingredients into the dry ingredients. Stir in 1 cup of peeled, grated dahlia tubers and ½ cup chopped black walnuts. Pour the batter into a greased loaf pan and bake at 350°F for about an hour. Test for doneness with a toothpick; when it comes clean from the center of the bread, remove the loaf from the oven and let cool.

## Acorn Brown Bread

In New England, empty baked bean cans are used to make a superb moist brown bread that's practically a meal on its own. Acorn flour takes this bread over the top, drops it on your plate, and says, "Eat me!"

In a bowl combine ½ cup cold-leached acorn flour, 1 cup whole wheat flour, 1 cup buttermilk, ½ teaspoon salt, 1 teaspoon baking soda, ⅜ cup molasses (not blackstrap; it's not quite sweet enough), and 1 cup chopped raisins. Remove one end cap from each of two 16-ounce baked bean cans, then clean the cans and grease them with butter or cooking spray. Fill each can three-quarters full and seal with aluminum foil fastened with a thick rubber band. Place the cans upright in a roasting pan, and pour water in the pan until it's almost full, but not so full you can't pick it up and move it without spilling! You should have at least 2 inches of water in the pan. Cook for 2 hours, checking at half-hour intervals and adding water to the pan if necessary. Then remove and let cool 10 minutes before sliding the bread out onto a

plate to finish cooling. With a little butter, the bread is dense, flavorful, and satisfying.

## Potage de Polygonum (a.k.a. knotweed soup)

Coarsely chop 1 pound of young knotweed stalks and 3 to 5 bulbs of field garlic. In a large pot, add the above to 4 cups of chicken or vegetable stock. Bring to a boil, then reduce heat and simmer for about 10 minutes, until everything is tender. Purée the mixture in a blender or food processor, then add ½ teaspoon dried dill or tarragon, and salt and pepper to taste. Return the soup to the pot and reheat. It should be slightly thinner than pea soup; if it's too thick, add more stock or a little water and stir. Serve hot, with a swirl of sour cream or yogurt.

## Acorn and Oyster Mushroom Soup

Chop and sauté 1 carrot, 1 celery stalk, and 1 medium onion in 2 tablespoons of butter until they soften. Rehydrate 1 ounce of dried oyster mushrooms (or 2½ cups fresh) and add them to the sautéed vegetables along with 1½ cups of acorn bits, either hot- or cold-leached. Stir to combine and sauté a few minutes more. Add 2 bay leaves (or 4 bayberry leaves or half a California bay leaf), 2 tablespoons sherry, and 2½ cups chicken or mushroom stock. Bring to a boil, then reduce heat and simmer for an hour, uncovered. Let the soup cool, then blend to purée and add salt to taste. Return to heat and, if it's too thick, thin with additional stock. Remove from the heat, pour into bowls, and stir

1 tablespoon of Greek yogurt into each bowl, then top with chopped parsley.

## Hortopita

*Pita* is the Greek word for pie, and *pites* (plural of *pita*) come in many flavors. There are sweet dessert pites and savory vegetable pites, individual appetizer pites stuffed with cheese, and meat pites that make a substantial main course. Almost every grocery store now carries phyllo dough in the dairy case, so making pita is no longer solely the purview of *yiayias* (Greek grandmothers) everywhere. Specialty stores may even carry country-style phyllo, which is slightly thicker than regular phyllo. While I prefer the thin stuff for baklava, I like the thicker, country-style dough for pita. If I can't find it, I use the thin phyllo and double up the internal layers.

This basic pita recipe replaces spinach with wild greens. Choose the greens according to your taste: mild, bitter, or a combination of both. Consider bishop's weed, garlic mustard, amaranth, Malabar spinach, purslane, and dandelion. Gather a pound of greens. It sounds like a lot, but greens cook down substantially so you'll need a full pound.

Chop 1 medium onion and cook it in butter or olive oil until it's soft. Add your greens, salt, pepper, and perhaps a little dried bee balm to taste, and cook until greens are fully reduced. Remove from the heat and stir in 1 cup of crumbled feta, 1 cup of cottage cheese or Greek yogurt, and 2 large eggs (beaten).

Unroll your phyllo, and cut it to fit a 9x13 baking pan. (Once the phyllo is unwrapped, be sure to keep it covered with a damp dish towel when you're not working with it, or else it will dry out and shatter if you look at it sideways.) Spray the pan with cooking spray. Some people may think this is anathema, but it saves *a lot* of time and produces a reduced-fat pita. If you can't bring yourself to use spray, you may brush with melted butter instead. I will allow it. Place a sheet of phyllo in the pan, then coat with butter or spray. Layer three more sheets, buttering or spraying each piece.

Spread some of the greens-cheese mixture onto the phyllo, creating a layer about a half-inch thick. Cover with one or two pieces of phyllo (depending on the thickness of your dough), and butter or spray each layer. Add more greens in another layer, and repeat the phyllo-greens alternation until all the greens are used up. Top with four layers of phyllo, spraying or buttering each piece of dough.

Bake in a 350°F oven for 35 to 45 minutes or until the top layer is golden brown. Let it cool to room temperature, then serve as either a side dish or main course.

## Mushroom Ravioli

Packaged won ton wrappers simplify this recipe, but if homemade pasta is something you love to make, feel free to do so. I think the thin won ton wrappers provide the perfect ratio of noodle to filling.

Slice 2 cups of assorted mushrooms and sauté them in a half stick of butter and 1 tablespoon of olive oil along with 3 cloves of garlic, also sliced. Cook until softened, then add salt and pepper to taste and ¼ cup mushroom broth. Cook over medium heat until the mixture cooks down and the liquid is mostly evaporated. Remove from the heat and let cool.

In a blender, combine 1½ cups ricotta cheese with 2 tablespoons grated parmesan, then add the cooled mushroom mixture and blend until smooth. If the mixture is too thick, add a little more broth, then fold in an additional ½ cup of chopped mushrooms. Taste and adjust seasoning if necessary.

Place 1 teaspoon of mushroom filling in the center of a won ton wrapper, then brush the edges of the wrapper with water and fold the wrapper in half diagonally, pressing the edges together to form a triangle. Make as many raviolis as you have filling for (any extra can be frozen for later use) and allow the stuffed pasta to air-dry for an hour. Boil briefly, until pasta is cooked through; this may only take 2 or 3 minutes. This is a delicate ravioli and will break apart if overstuffed or overcooked.

After draining the pasta, serve and top with a butter-and-sage sauce, or whatever else your little heart desires. Crazy good.

# Fruity Miscellany

Here are a few additional ways to use fruit juices or pulps. *Agua fresca* — an icy, slushy, fruit drink — is simplicity in itself. Fruit fool is a sophisticated British dessert made from fruit pulp. Fruit pudding falls somewhere in between on the time-complexity continuum. All are wonderful, refreshing ways to take advantage of summer's harvest.

## Aronia *Agua Fresca*

Place 2 cups of aronia juice in a blender with a handful of ice cubes and 2 teaspoons of agave nectar. Purée and pour into martini glasses, then bottoms up. *¡Que fresca!* Pineapple guava also makes a tasty *agua fresca*.

## Silverberry Pudding

This basic recipe works with any mashed berry or fruit pulp, although you may need to adjust the amount of sugar according to the sweetness of the fruit.

In a shallow pan, barely cover your fruit with water and simmer to soften. Run through a food mill to remove seeds. (If you're using a fruit with small seeds, like Juneberries, you can skip the food mill and just pulp the berries in a blender.) In a saucepan, combine 2 cups of pulp with ⅓ cup of sugar and 3 tablespoons of instant tapioca and let it sit for 5 minutes. Bring to a full boil over medium heat, stirring regularly. Let cool 20 minutes, then stir and pour into serving dishes. Serve warm or cold, according to your taste.

If you prefer to use homemade arrowroot or canna starch for this pudding, make a paste by combining 1 tablespoon arrowroot powder with 1 tablespoon water. Set this aside. In a saucepan over medium heat, whisk together the fruit and sugar until it comes to a boil. Add the arrowroot paste and whisk until the mixture begins to simmer, then remove from heat and pour into serving dishes. This version will need several hours in the refrigerator to set.

## Cornelian Cherry Fool

Classic fool recipes call for gooseberries, currants, or raspberries, but cornelian cherries make a delicious, refreshing dessert that will have everyone guessing about its flavor. Mix 2 cups cornelian cherry pulp with ¾ cup sugar in a shallow pan and whisk to combine. Remove from heat.

In a bowl, whip 1 cup heavy cream, then fold in ¾ cup Greek yogurt. Add 1 tablespoon lemon juice, 1 tablespoon white wine, and half the cornelian cherry mixture; combine well. Spoon this mixture into parfait glasses and refrigerate. Just before serving, pour the remaining fruit/sugar mixture on top of the fruit/yogurt mixture and serve. The combination of creamy and tart is unbelievably delicious. I can't get enough.

## Rose Hip Soup (a.k.a. *nyponsoppa*)

There is no denying the elegance of a cold, smooth fruit soup. In Sweden, *nyponsoppa* is traditionally served for dessert; similar soups are popular throughout Scandinavia and Eastern Europe. This recipe highlights the sweet/tart flavor of rose hips and calls for no additional spices or flavors. It's a great way to get acquainted with the pure taste of rose hips, which is difficult to describe: mostly fruity with a touch of the vegetal.

Combine 2 cups of rose hip purée, 2 cups of water, and ⅛ to ¼ cup sugar over low heat and stir to dissolve the sugar. (I recommend starting with less sugar and adjusting it according to your taste as you cook.) Separately, mix 1 tablespoon cornstarch with 1 tablespoon cold water to create a paste. Whisk the paste into the rose hip base and stir over medium heat until the soup begins to thicken. The soup may be allowed to simmer slightly, but be sure to keep stirring to avoid scorching it.

When the soup has reached the desired thickness, remove it from the heat and refrigerate to cool. To serve, swirl in whipped cream or pour it over vanilla ice cream. A few crunchy cookies, like gingersnaps or almond biscotti, are the perfect garnish for this richly colored and flavored soup.

# RESOURCES AND RECOMMENDED READING

One book cannot be all things to all readers. If this book has made you want to know more about foraging, wild edible plants, or preserving food, here are some of my favorite books you might consider adding to your library. I find myself going back to them again and again.

## Books about Wild Edible Plants

Once you're familiar with the edible plants in your own backyard, why not look for wild edibles farther afield? The best way to get acquainted with wild edibles is to tag along at the feet of a master (or mistress). If you don't have a wise old granny to school you, find a class or walking tour where you can get hands-on education. And you might want to read everything you can get your hands on. I know I would.

*The Forager's Harvest* (Forager's Harvest, 2006)
*Nature's Garden* (Forager's Harvest, 2010)

**Both by Samuel Thayer**

Thayer is one of today's leading foragers, and his books combine vast personal experience with solid research. Plus he has strong opinions and a wicked sense of humor, which makes his prose especially memorable. Outstanding color photography shows plants at various stages of development and in situ, giving readers insight into where to find wild edibles and how to prepare the harvest. Thayer's books aren't encyclopedias. They focus on a select group of plants and go into tremendous detail for each one. You can truly learn a plant and make it your own by using Thayer's books as your guide.

*Edible Wild Plants: Wild Foods from Dirt to Plate* (Gibbs Smith, 2010)

**By John Kallas**

Kallas is up there with Thayer at the head of this field. The first in a series, this volume includes 18 plants, primarily greens, and describes them exhaustively. Like Thayer, Kallas writes from years of personal experience, and his book is comprehensively researched. His photographs are excellent, and he includes detailed nutritional information on each recommended plant.

*Stalking the Blue-Eyed Scallop* (D. McKay, 1964)
*Stalking the Healthful Herbs* (D. McKay, 1966)
*Stalking the Wild Asparagus* (50th anniversary ed., A.C. Hood, 2012)

**All by Euell Gibbons**

Gibbons was the world's most famous forager for a reason. His writing is engaging and personal and reads like a memoir. You can't use these books as field guides; it's difficult to identify plants without photography or detailed drawings. But you can look to them for general information on seasonal harvests and inspiration in the kitchen. Gibbons was passionate about edible plants, and his enthusiasm was contagious. He was also an excellent storyteller.

*The Edible Wild* (Pagurian Press, 1971)

**By Berndt Berglund and Clare E. Bolsby**

My sister found this book in a used bookstore and bought it for me for 25¢. It's worth 100 times the price. Published in 1971, the book is illustrated with a few excellent line drawings. It's chock-full of recipes that are both unusual and compelling. Do you need to taste stewed milkweed pods with frogs' legs? Because I kind of do. As I write this, there are 13 copies available on Amazon. Run, do not walk.

*Wild Plants I Have Known . . . and Eaten* (Essex County Greenbelt Association, 2004)

**By Russ Cohen**

This is a small book that focuses on plants found in and around Massachusetts, where the author is a popular wild-foods teacher. With small black-and-white images, it isn't exactly a field guide, but the plant descriptions are excellent and often contain unusual trivia and history that make the plants all the more memorable. Cohen also includes information on the rarity of wild edible plants and whether they can be collected without damaging plant populations.

# Foraging Books and Blogs

I first read the following two authors online. Both have informative, well-illustrated blogs full of practical information. Their books are more memoir than field guide. Although they provide thorough descriptions of many plants, there are no detailed illustrations to help with identification. This is not a shortcoming! Both books are enjoyable, provocative reads that will motivate a burgeoning forager to experiment and explore.

*Hunt, Gather, Cook* (Rodale, 2011)
Hunter Angler Gardener Cook
*honest-food.net*

**By Hank Shaw**

I don't have the heart to hunt, but I respect those who do it well, and by "well" I mean with respect, competence, and safety. I believe Shaw is one of those hunters. His writing style is humorous and detail-oriented. I enjoy reading his chapters on hunting and fishing even though I don't practice either of these things myself. His foraging brings together both East Coast and West Coast experience, and his recipes are sophisticated and delicious. I often look to him for inspiration and instruction.

*Fat of the Land* (Skipstone, 2009)
Fat of the Land
*fat-of-the-land.blogspot.com*

**By Langdon Cook**

This book reads like a collection of short stories, each chapter a complete tale involving a specific time, place, and wild food. Cook writes about plants, mushrooms, seafood, and the friends and family he forages with. Each chapter ends with a recipe and leaves you with the feeling that you've just had an adventure.

Eat the Weeds
*eattheweeds.com*

Green Deane hasn't published a foraging book, but his website is chock-full of excellent information, including recipes. He also has *lots* of very helpful how-to videos, all available for free.

# Mushrooms

The thrill that accompanies a fabulous fungal find is enough to cause grown women to jump up and down like children. Fortunately, many people share my obsession, and there are mycological clubs and societies around the world. The North American Mycological Association (NAMA, namyco.org) can connect you to like-minded mycophiles in your area.

*The Complete Mushroom Hunter: An Illustrated Guide to Finding, Harvesting, and Enjoying Wild Mushrooms* (Quarry Books, 2010)

**By Gary Lincoff**

Gary Lincoff is a walking encyclopedia. This book is perfect for beginning mushroom hunters for several reasons: clear documentary photography; an engaging writing style; and easy, tasty recipes. He describes a manageable number of safe mushrooms, and he encourages the reader to start small and slow, getting to know a few new species at a time. He also includes information on medicinal mushrooms and poisonous species to avoid. Once you've mastered the mushrooms in this book, you can graduate to the *National Audubon Society Field Guide to North American Mushrooms,* which Lincoff also authored.

*100 Edible Mushrooms* (University of Michigan Press, 2007)

**By Michael Kuo**

*Edible Wild Mushrooms of North America: A Field-to-Kitchen Guide* (University of Texas Press, 1992)

**By David W. Fischer and Alan E. Bessette**

When you read Gary Lincoff's book, you'll feel like you're walking in the woods with a knowledgeable friend. The two titles listed above are slightly less personal in their narrative tone, but they are excellent resources nonetheless. They include identification information and recipe suggestions for approximately 100 edible mushroom species. If you decide to delve more deeply into wild mushroom hunting, I suggest both of them.

# Vendors of Mushroom-Growing Supplies

If you'd like to try cultivating mushrooms at home (indoors or out), these vendors sell kits that can get you started.

Field & Forest Products, Inc.
**800-792-6220**
*fieldforest.net*

Fungi Perfecti
**800-780-9126**
*fungi.com*

Mushroom Adventures
**530-741-2437**
*mushroomadventures.com*

# Food Preparation

The harvest is in. What are you going to do with it? Whether you cook your backyard bounty right away or save it for later culinary capers, there are some specialty skills that may come in handy.

*Ball Blue Book Guide to Preserving* (100th anniversary ed., Jarden Home Brands, 2010)

It's a slim volume, and the first book I bought when I decided to start preserving my own food. I refer to it often, more for techniques and canning times than for recipes, although for the beginner the recipe suggestions are generally solid. This is an excellent place to start.

*Putting Food By* (5th ed., Penguin, 2010)
**By Janet Greene, Ruth Hertzberg, and Beatrice Vaughan**

When you've explored the *Ball Blue Book*, the next natural step is *Putting Food By*. It contains detailed information on a variety of preserving techniques; it explains how they work and why they sometimes fail. The authors recommend different methods for different foods, including general techniques and numerous recipes. Some of the information in the older editions is slightly outdated, so look for the newest revision.

*Making Wild Wines & Meads: 125 Unusual Recipes Using Herbs, Fruits, Flowers, and More* (Storey Publishing, 1999)
**By Pattie Vargas and Rich Gulling**

This book is my winemaking bible. It's a primer for the beginner, describing the basic equipment, the science of fermentation, and the general steps and timetable of making wine. The recipes range from simple apple wine to more complex honey-flower-herb combinations. It literally contains everything you need to know to get started, and then some.

*On Food and Cooking* (rev ed., Scribner, 2004)
**By Harold McGee**

If you want to know *how* and *why,* buy this book. It's not specifically about wild foods, nor is it a recipe book, but if you want to understand how pectin molecules form chains or why salt is an effective food preservative, this is the book for you. As a reference, it deserves a place on every serious cook's bookshelf. As a bedside read, its 800+ pages will keep you busy for a long time.

# INTERIOR PHOTOGRAPHY

## Interior Photography Credits

© Rob Cardillo: 1, 2, 5 border, 8, 10 border, 11, 12, 17–19, 21–23, 25 (jelly bag), 26 (dehydrator), 28 border, 29–33, 35, 38–40, 43–47, 49, 51, 53, 55–58, 59 right, 60–62, 64, 65, 67–74, 77, 78 border, 79–84, 86–89, 91, 93–101, 104, 105 top, 106–109, 112, 116–119, 121, 123, 124, 128, 129 top, 130, 132, 133, 134 border, 135–137, 138 top, 139, 140, 142 left, 143–149, 151 bottom, 152 border, 153, 155–157, 160, 163–165, 166 right, 167–171, 172 border, 173–184, 185 top, 186–189, 191, 193 left, 206 border, 207, 211–217, 219, 224, 229, and 230

## Additional photography by

© allocricetulus/iStockphoto.com: 25 (knife)

© David Cavagnaro: 154

© Ellen Zachos: 15, 37, 41, 42, 52, 59 left, 63, 85, 90, 92, 103, 105 bottom, 110, 111 right, 113–115, 120, 122, 125–127, 138 bottom, 141, 142 right, 150, 151 top, 158, 159, 162, 166 left, 185 bottom, 190 border, 193 bottom right, 195, 201, 202, 209, 210, and 218

© Erik Hoffner: 193 top right, 203, and 204

© GAP Photos, Ltd./Howard Rice: 131

© ginosphotos/iStockphoto.com: 5 and throughout (paper texture) and 25 (paper bag)

© Graham Taylor/Dreamstime.com: 26 (jars)

© hocus-focus/iStockphoto.com: 13 and throughout (note paper)

© Iakov Filimonov/Dreamstime.com: 26 (spice grinder)

© Kristy Rustay: 197

© Marco Mayer/Dreamstime.com: 25 (food mill)

Mars Vilaubi: 27 (canner)

© Neil Hardwick/Alamy: 198

© Robert McLean/Alamy: 27 (pressure canner)

© Rosemary Kautzky: 102

© RT Images/iStockphoto.com: 24 (fork and spade)

R.W. Smith, Lady Bird Johnson Wildlife Center: 129 bottom left and right

© Saxon Holt: 36 and 111 left

© Yuri Minaev/iStockphoto.com: 24 (pruners)

# INDEX

Page numbers in *italics* indicate photographs and tables.

# H

habitats, plants and, 12–15
harvesting, 16–27
    ethical, 14
hawthorn (*Crataegus* species), 88–89, *88, 89*
hedgehog *Hydrum repardum, H. umbilicatum*), 198–99, *198*
    ready for dehydrator, *209*
hemlock needles, 29
hen-of-the-woods (*Grifola frondosa*), *23,* 200–1, *201*
herbaceous plants, 28–77
highbush cranberry (*Viburnum trilobum*), 90–91, *90, 91*
hips
    rose, rugosa (*Rosa rugosa*), 120–21, *120*
    Rose Hip Soup, 223
hopniss (*Apios americana*), *8, 13,* 158–61, *158, 159, 160*
horse chestnut, 142, *142*
Hortopita, 221
hosta (*Hosta* species), 18, 44–45, *44, 45*

# J

inulin, 157, 165
invasive plants. *See also* weeds
    bamboo (*Phyllostachys* species), 30–31
    garlic mustard (*Allaria petiolata*), 42–43, *42, 43*

# J

jams, 212–16
    Juneberry Jam, 215–16

Japanese chestnut. *See* chestnut
Japanese knotweed (*Fallopia japonica, Polygonum cuspidatum*), 13, 46–47, *46, 47*
    Potage de Polygonum, 220
J-choke. *See* Jerusalem artichoke
jellies, 212–16
    testing for jell point, 215, *215*
    jelly bag and stand, 25, *25*
    Mountain Ash Jelly, 213–15, *213, 214, 215*
jelly bag and stand, 25, *25*
Jerusalem artichoke (*Helianthus tuberosus*), 162–65, *162, 163, 164, 165*
Joseph's coat (*Amaranthus tricolor*), 48, *49*
Juneberry (*Amelanchier* species), 12, 19, 94–95, *94, 95*
    Juneberry Jam, 215–16
juniper (*Juniperus communis*), 96–97, *96, 97*

# K

kousa dogwood (*Cornus kousa*), 98–99, *98, 99*

# L

lakes, plants and, 13
landscapes, assessing for edibles, 12–13
lawns, plants and, 12
leaf node, *18*
leaves, edible, 28–77. *See also* foliage

bee balm (*Monarda didyma, M. fistulosa*), 32, *32, 33*
bishop's weed (*Aegopodium podagraria*), 34—35, *35*
California bay (*Umbellularia californica*), 36–37, *36*
chameleon plant (*Houttynia cordata* 'Chameleon' and other varieties), 38–39, *38, 39*
chickweed (*Stellaria media*), 40–41, *40, 41*
daisy, oxeye (*Leucanthemum vulgare, Chrysanthemum lecanthemum*), 60–61, *60, 61*
dandelion (*Taraxacum officinale*), 174–77, *177*
freezing, 208
garlic mustard (*Alliaria petiolata*), 42–43, *42, 43*
harvesting, 18
hawthorn (*Crataegus* species), 88–89, *89*
Joseph's coat (*Amaranthus tricolor*), 48
lotus (*Nelumbo nucifera, N. lutea*), 166–67, *166*
Malabar spinach (*Basella alba*), 50, *51*
miner's lettuce (*Claytonia perfoliata, Montia perfoliata*), 12, 13, 15, 18, 52–53, *52, 53*
mulberry (*Morus* species), 106–7, *106, 107*
nasturtium (*Tropaeolum majus*), 54, *55*

# S

# y

# Cultivate Your Kitchen Creativity
## with More Books from Storey

**edited by Carleen Madigan**

This comprehensive guide to self-sufficiency has all the information you need to grow and preserve vegetables, fruits, herbs, nuts, and grains; raise a variety of animals for meat and dairy; keep honey bees; and much more.

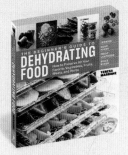

**by Teresa Marrone**

Stock your pantry with dried foods for year-round enjoyment. Detailed, yet accessible, instructions for using a table-top dehydrator or harnessing the power of the sun teach you how to make apple rings, kale chips, fruit leather, and even baby food.

**by Matthew Weingarten & Raquel Pelzel**

Forage wild ingredients from the sea, forests, and rivers, and preserve them in your own kitchen using old-world methods. Dozens of delicious recipes teach you how to cure, can, smoke, and pickle your foraged bounty.

**by Ellen Zachos**

Create delicious mixed drinks using common flowers, berries, and roots. Get your party started with more than 50 recipes for garnishes, syrups, juices, and bitters, then use your handcrafted components in cocktails such as Stinger in the Rye, Don't Sass Me, and Tree-tini.

**Join the conversation.** Share your experience with this book, learn more about Storey Publishing's authors, and read original essays and book excerpts at *storey.com*. Look for our books wherever quality books are sold or call 800-441-5700.